Grade 1 Teacher's Guide

EVERY DAY COUNTS®
CALENDAR MATH

Janet G. Gillespie

Patsy F. Kanter

GReaT SOuRCe®
EDUCATION GROUP
A Houghton Mifflin Company
New Ways to Know®

ACKNOWLEDGMENTS

We offer special thanks to

- **our mentors:** the late Mary Baratta-Lorton, Marilyn Burns, Andy Clark, Jay Greenwood, Constance Kamii, Ruby Payne, Kathy Richardson, Allyn Snider, and the late Robert Wirtz for inspiring and guiding our work in the classroom through their workshops and writing.
- **our families:** Tim, Nathan, and Josh Gillespie; and David, Julie, and Nathan Kanter for making our lives count every day and without whose support none of this could have been written.
- **our contributing author:** Beth Ardell for her vision and expertise.
- **our parents:** Nat and Louise Friedler and Ragnar and Anna Giske for being our first teachers and for believing in us and valuing our work as teachers.
- **the Great Source team:** Evelyn Curley, Betsy Donaghey, Rick Duthe, Kathy Kellman, Susan Rogalski, and Richard Spencer for making this edition of *Every Day Counts®* *Calendar Math* a reality.

CREDITS

Cover design: Kristen Davis, Great Source
Cover art: Amy Vangsgard & Kristen Davis
Design: Taurins Design
Electronic art: Taurins Design

Printed in China

Great Source®, Every Day Counts®, and *New Ways to Know®* are registered trademarks of Houghton Mifflin Company.

International Standard Book Number-10: 0-669-51440-3

International Standard Book Number-13: 978-0-669-51440-7

5 6 7 8 9 10 - RRDS - 09 08 07

TABLE OF CONTENTS

Dear Fellow Teachers,

We are so glad that you have chosen *Every Day Counts® Calendar Math* for your classroom. For our new users, welcome and for our veteran users, thanks for your continued confidence in and support for *Every Day Counts Calendar Math*.

Every Day Counts Calendar Math is built on our many years of classroom experience teaching mathematics. An interactive K-6 supplemental mathematics program, *Every Day Counts Calendar Math* is designed to capitalize on daily discussions to foster children's mathematical confidence and competence. The program is based on our observations from our years of teaching and is supported by research that shows:

1. Children need to learn mathematics incrementally, giving them the opportunity to develop understandings over time.

2. Visual models help children visualize and verbalize number and geometric relationships.

3. Classroom discussion fosters the growth of language acquisition and development of reasoning. It also allows children to discover that there are many strategies for solving problems.

4. Over time, children can learn to think algebraically. Early exposure to this type of thinking will lead them to a successful future in mathematics.

5. Observing and listening to children is essential to ongoing assessment that can guide instruction.

This edition of *Every Day Counts Calendar Math* has new features to reduce your workload, and new elements to increase the level of success for your students. The Teacher's Guide is organized to aid instruction: **Concepts and Skills** tell the focus of each lesson, **Author Notes** explain the thinking behind the elements, **Materials** and **Setup** list preparation tips, and **Daily Routine** outlines the update procedure. As always **Discussion** offers questions and sample dialogues to help guide your lessons, and **Helpful Hints** further enrich the lessons. New to this edition are **Ongoing Assessment** questions that reveal individual children's knowledge and help you to meet different students' instructional needs. Ongoing Assessment also appears in a separate booklet in the kit for easy use during Calendar time.

The kit contains the usual materials needed to get started—counting tape paper, a Calendar, Calendar Pieces for each month, month strips, yesterday, today, and tomorrow markers for grades K–2, demo coins, play money for grades 3–5, and plastic pockets. New to this kit are some background posters to arrange the bulletin board with ease, Counting Tape Pieces to count the days in school, manipulatives, paper clips to get the calendars ready for immediate use, and storage bags.

We have learned much from our teaching colleagues and appreciate their support, suggestions and the opportunities to teach together. Most of all we offer our thanks to our main teachers—the children throughout the country with whom we've had the privilege to work, and who have taught us so much. Best wishes to you as you teach math this year and in years to come.

Collegially,

Janet Gillespie   *Patsy F. Kanter*

Every Day Counts® Calendar Math appeals to the natural way children learn math—building on concepts a little at a time, every day. Simple to use, the Teacher's Guide and kit contain a full year of activities with suggestions for discussions that will have your students excited about "talking math."

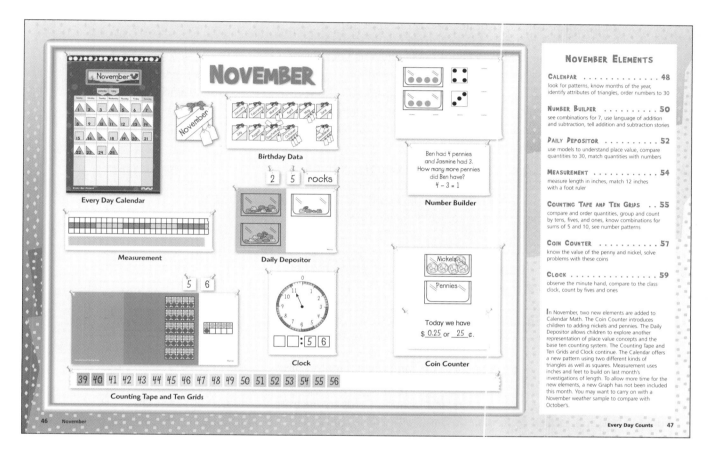

A lot of math in a little time. In just 10–15 minutes a day, *Every Day Counts* provides supplemental math instruction that revolves around a simple interactive bulletin board with a variety of elements, or components. As children build the bulletin board, they also build mathematical understanding and confidence. Great progress is made in small incremental steps.

Children learn from their discoveries. Students' observations and thinking are the driving force behind *Every Day Counts.* Different monthly elements provide a continuous learning experience in which students examine mathematical relationships central to the curriculum for their grade level. This daily, visual, hands-on exposure to critical math concepts complements the natural way children learn—building on concepts a little at a time, every day, to help them develop mathematical competence and confidence.

"The EDC board was a hit with my kids because it was interactive and it was not from a book. It was almost difficult to convince them that it was math! It dovetailed into so many areas that the book covers anyway, it was either a great introduction or a great review for many concepts."

Linda Hoerling-Glenn
Teacher, Tacoma, WA

Classroom discussion: the heart of *Every Day Counts*. With the discussion questions that are provided for a variety of levels, children use mathematical language to explain their thinking in the common "folk language" of math such as "I had 5 marbles and I got 3 more, and now I have 8." Asking students to share the various ways they arrived at answers helps them see that

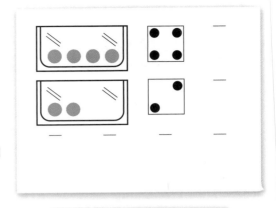

- There are many ways to work with numbers
- There is more than one way to approach a problem
- The same way of working out a problem may be explained in several different ways. '

As Calendar Math conversations continue and grow in depth throughout the year, children begin to use formal math language in context and with increasing confidence and familiarity. The vocabulary makes sense to them and becomes part of their knowledge.

Help for struggling learners. Incremental changes in the bulletin board allow English Language Learners and struggling math students to build skills and understanding at a comfortable rate. If understanding does not come immediately, there is always another day.

Six kids were playing in the park and 2 went home. How many kids were still playing?
6 − 2 = 4

Number Builder

A mathematical kaleidoscope. With *Every Day Counts,* each day is slightly different from the day before. As students build on each of the elements, new relationships are examined and discussed. In Grade 1 the following elements encourage children to explore a year's worth of math concepts and skills:

- **The Calendar** presents a unique pattern of colors or geometric shapes each month as one new Calendar Piece is added each day. Children develop patterning and reasoning skills as they predict what the next piece will be.
- **The Counting Tape and Ten Grids** keeps track of the number of days of school as one new numbered square is added to the Tape and one dot is filled in on a Ten Grid each school day. Children develop number sense, place value concepts, and mental math skills as the numbers grow from 1 to 180.
- **Number Builder** uses plastic counters and Domino Cards to illustrate addition and subtraction concepts and basic fact families, and to encourage children to connect number stories with number sentences.
- **Daily Depositor** reinforces place value concepts as a variety of objects are collected for each day of the month and bundled into tens as the quantity grows to 30 or 31.
- **Clock** gives children daily practice reading analog and digital displays, and helps them focus first on the minute hand and then both hands together while developing vocabulary of elapsed time.
- **Coin Counter** collects one penny every day of the month, familiarizing children with the value of pennies, nickels, dimes, and quarters and offering opportunities to find equivalencies and make trades with ease.
- **Measurement** helps children experience the language of estimation, comparing and measuring using standard and nonstandard units of length, capacity, and weight.
- **Graph** offers children the opportunity to collect, graph, and analyze a variety of data such as weather records or the results of classroom preference polls and probability experiments.

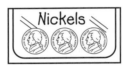

Today we have
$ 0.18 or 18 ¢.

Coin Counter

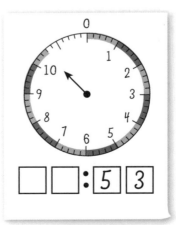

Clock

A Comprehensive Teacher's Guide. The Teacher's Guide for each grade level of *Every Day Counts* is organized by month and by elements. Each month begins with a picture of what the bulletin board might look like toward the middle of the month. A brief overview of suggested elements and activities for the month follows. As each element is introduced, you will find:

- **Concepts & Skills** for that activity

- A list of **Materials** for the activities, all either in the kit or readily available like paper clips

- The **Daily Routine** provides an easy-to-follow explanation of how to present this month's activities

- **Discussions** offer suggestions for discussion and assessment as well as sample dialogues

- **Helpful Hints** to share ideas such as games, literature, or extensions of the month's activities. Many of these hints originated with teachers using *Calendar Math* in their classrooms.

Key math **vocabulary** terms are highlighted where they are first introduced and are also defined and illustrated in the Teacher Resource section.

ONGOING ASSESSMENT TOOLS

- The **Ongoing Assessment** booklet provides an organized list of suggested assessment questions for use with each month's activities. These questions may also be used as a quick reference guide to instruction on days that time is limited.

- Each month **Ongoing Assessment** questions for each element are provided in the Teacher's Guide to help you gain insight into children's developing mathematical thinking.

- The teacher's everyday role is that of observer, listener, recorder, and questioner. Through daily observations and listening to children's discussions, assessment is ongoing.

- Assessment copy masters in the Teacher's Guide provide an easy way to capture progress at significant points of the year. A pretest for the beginning of the year allows you to assess children's prior knowledge. Two interim tests and a post test for the end of the year help you to gauge growth of understanding.

Every Day Counts® Calendar Math **is supported by research and practice.** Research shows that continuous exposure to critical math concepts allows children to develop an understanding of important mathematical concepts over time and to learn at an individual pace. Experience from classroom practice demonstrates that young children actively, incrementally construct mathematical knowledge. Understanding is solidified through reflection on real-life data, group discussion, and cooperative problem solving. The topics and challenges at each grade are aligned with NCTM standards and build on what students learn in class with activities that engage students, allowing them to explore, make and test conjectures, and apply their mathematics. Students using *Every Day Counts® Calendar Math* have been shown to develop higher-level thinking skills, enjoy math more, see its application in the real world, and score higher on standardized tests.

There is little preparation for *Every Day Counts Calendar Math*. Once the materials are prepared and organized, your prep work for the year is minimal.

The following materials will be very useful in organizing and preparing the materials in your kit: a roll of masking tape; a craft knife; a box of bulletin board push pins; a sheet of 11" × 17" construction paper or other heavy paper.

PREPARING THE POSTERS

Many teachers have found that a "slit and clip" method works best to attach the Calendar Pieces and other kit items to the Calendar, Daily Depositor, and Ten Grids posters. To prepare the Calendar use a craft knife to place a half-inch cut at the top of each space on the Calendar. You'll find a hairline rule at the top of each space to show you where to make the slit. Insert a small paper clip in each slit. Each Calendar Piece will slide beneath a clip. This "slit-and-clip" method makes it easy for both you and the children to put the pieces on and take them off for counting. It also allows you to place the Calendar on a wall or other surface that doesn't accept push pins. To secure the paper clips, put strips of masking tape over the paper clips on the back of the Calendar. Use the same technique on the Ten Grids and the Daily Depositor posters.

Calendar

PREPARING THE COUNTING TAPE

Use the roll of adding machine tape in the kit to create the base of the Counting Tape. Cut a piece of adding machine tape 4–5 feet long and attach it to the wall above your bulletin board. You will use the colored paper squares included in the kit to build the Counting Tape throughout the school year. To make the Counting Tape continuous, add additional sections of adding machine tape as needed throughout the year.

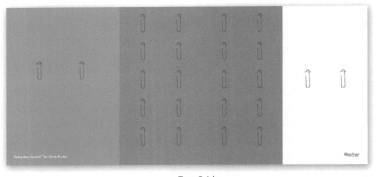

Ten Grids

PREPARING NUMBER BUILDER

Use the sheet of 11" × 17" construction paper to make the background for Number Builder. With the paper in the landscape position, cut 3 rows of 4 paper clip slits, spaced about $3\frac{1}{2}$" apart both horizontally and vertically. Insert 12 paper clips and put strips of masking tape over the paper clips on the back of the paper. For September clip two clear pockets to the left-hand side of the mat.

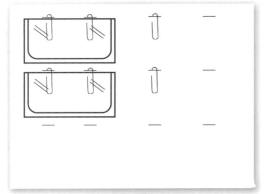

Number Builder

ORGANIZING THE CARDSTOCK

You have a set of cardstock Calendar Pieces for the Calendar that are organized and labeled by month. Carefully punch out a set (three sheets) for each month. Put each month's pieces in the resealable plastic bags and label them with the name of the month. Punch out the Today Arrow Marker and store it with your first month's Calendar Pieces.

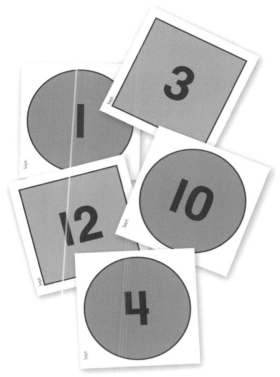

September Calendar Pieces

CHOOSING AMONG THE POSSIBILITIES

Flip to the beginning of each month in this Teacher's Guide and scan through the range of elements that make up *Every Day Counts* at your grade level. The first year you might want to start small and limit the number of elements you share with the class. Your preparation can be minimized, and your primary focus can be facilitating class discussions. Begin with the year-long elements—the Counting Tape and Ten Grids, the Number Builder, and the Calendar. You might also choose an element that provides experience with a topic students have had difficulty with in the past. As the year goes by and you become familiar with the program, you may choose to add new elements to further enrich your discussions.

ARRANGING THE EDC BULLETIN BOARD DISPLAY

Choose a place in your room where you can create a bulletin board that is easily accessible to you and your students. Many teachers who use *Every Day Counts* do not hang everything in one location. Sometimes Graphs are placed across the room or the Counting Tape is hung under the chalkboard. Some teachers choose an area where children can gather together on the floor to hold daily class meetings to make updates to the bulletin board.

PLANNING CLASS TIME

We recommend that the EDC discussion last for only 10–15 minutes each day. In order to stay within this time period all displays are updated, but only 1–2 elements are discussed. A quick update of the Counting Tape in Grade 3 might flow like this:

Teacher: Yesterday we had been in school 47 days. How many days have we been in school as of today?

Class: 48.

Teacher: Will today's square be pink or yellow?

Class: Yellow because 48 is an even number.

This simple update takes less than 30 seconds. If the Counting Tape is to be discussed, an extended series of questions might be asked, such as:

- What day will it be in three days?
- How did you figure out that answer?
- Talk to us about a pattern you see on the Counting Tape.

If a special occasion means you will not have time for any EDC discussion, at least commit to keeping the display updated so the elements are always current.

CUSTOMIZING YOUR PLANS

Every classroom runs on a different schedule. You may have special events, field trips, or snow days that change your daily routine. To help you keep track of the concepts you want to cover with *Every Day Counts Calendar Math,* we have provided a simple planner copy master that you can use to organize your plans.

EDC WEEKLY PLANNER

	MONDAY Date: Nov 16 Day in School: 47	TUESDAY Date: Nov 17 Day in School: 48	WEDNESDAY Date: Nov 18 Day in School: 49	THURSDAY Date: Nov 19 Day in School: 50	FRIDAY Date: Nov 20 Day in School: 51 new pocket for Depositor
Materials to Prepare	None		CT & Ten Grids—days till day 50	CT & Ten Grids—half of hundred! Clock—count by fives, tens	Calendar—predict Monday Depositor—a new group of ten
Element to Discuss	Calendar—predict tomorrow Coin counter—3 nickels + 1	Number Builder – list all the ways to make 7 Measurement—17 inches			
Concepts to Focus on	predicting, counting by fives, counting on	take away and comparing, estimating	one more	groups of ten, count by tens, doubles and half	predicting, place value, groups of ten
Children to Observe	Tia—let her trade coins	Sarah –a comparing story? LaToya—can she count on to Day 50?	Matt—what will tomorrow's number be?	Sean, Katie—do they understand half of 50? half of 100?	Jon— have him count by tens
Special Days				Halfway to 100!	

Every Day Counts 11

© Great Source. Copying is permitted; see page ii.

10 Customizing Your Plans

© Great Source. Copying is prohibited.

EDC WEEKLY PLANNER

	MONDAY Date: ____ Day in School: ____	TUESDAY Date: ____ Day in School: ____	WEDNESDAY Date: ____ Day in School: ____	THURSDAY Date: ____ Day in School: ____	FRIDAY Date: ____ Day in School: ____
Materials to Prepare					
Element to Discuss					
Concepts to Focus on					
Children to Observe					
Special Days					

Numbers & Operations	Aug/Sept	Oct	Nov	Dec	Jan	Feb	Mar	April	May/June
compose & decompose numbers	N	N	CT, D, N	CC, CT, D, N	CT, D, N	C, CT, D, H, N	CT, N	CT, N	N
understand place value		CT	CT, D	CC, CT, D	CC, CT, D	CT, D	CT, D	CT, N	CT, N
compare & order numbers	C, CT, G, N	C, CT	C, CT, D	C, CT, D	C, CC, CT, D	CC, CT, D, H	C, CT	C, CT	C, CT
count with one-to-one correspondence	C, G, N	C, CT, G, N	C, D, N	C, CT, D, N	C, CT, D, N	C, CT, D, H, N	C, CT, M, N	C, N	C, N
relate number words & numerals to quantities	C, CT, N	C, CT, N	C, CT, D, N	C, CC, CT, D, N	C, CT, D, N	C, CT, D, H, N	C, CT, M, N	C, CT	C, CT, N
understand ordinal numbers	C	N	N	N			C		
read numerals	C, CL, CT, G	C, CL, CT	C, CT, D	C, CT, D	C, CT, D	C, CT, D, H	C, CT	C, CT	C, CT
write numerals	CT	CT	CT, D	CT, D	CT, D	CT, D	CT	CT	CT
explore part/whole relationships	N	C, N	D, N	D, N	D, N	CT, D, H, N	N	N	N
use odd & even numbers			CT	CT		C, G		N	
addition concepts	N	CT, N	CC, CT, D, N	CC, CT, D, N	N	C, CT, D, N	C, CC, CT, N	CT, N	CT, N
subtraction concepts	N	CT, N	CT, D, N	CT, D, N	N	N	N	N	N
relate addition and subtraction	N	CT, N	CT, N	N	N	N	N	N	N
equal groupings/ equal shares			C	CT, D		CT, H			
compare quantities	N	CT, N	CT, D, N	CC, CT, N	N	C, CT, N	CT, N	N	N
number sense/ number patterns	C, CT, N	C, CT	C, CT	C, CT, D	C, CT, N	C, CT, N	CT	C, CT	C, CT
unit fractions			CT			C			
decimals w/ money amounts			CC	CC	CC	CC	CC, CL	CC	CC
count by 2, 5, or 10	CL, N	CL, CT	C, CL, CT	CL, CT	CL, CT	C, CC, CL, CT, G, H		CC, CT	CT
addition strategies	N	CT, N	CT, D, N	CT, D, N	D, N	CT, D, H, N	CC, CT, N	CT, N	CT, N
subtraction strategies	N	CT, N	CT, D, N	CT, D, N	D, N	CT, D, H, N	N	N	N

KEY

C = CALENDAR
CC = COIN COUNTER
CL = CLOCK
CT = COUNTING TAPE & TEN GRIDS
D = DAILY DEPOSITOR
G = GRAPH
H = ONE HUNDREDTH DAY CELEBRATION
M = MEASUREMENT
N = NUMBER BUILDER

Numbers & Operations (Continued)	Aug/Sept	Oct	Nov	Dec	Jan	Feb	Mar	April	May/June
counting on or back	N, CT	CT	CT	C, CC, CT, D	C, CT	C, CT, D, H	CT	CC, CT	CT
basic facts/ number stories	N	CT, N	T, N	CC, CT, D, N	N	CT, D, H	N	N	CT, N
regrouping to add or subtract			CT		D	D			N
add/subtract double digits			CT	CT	CT	CT	CT	CT	CT
multiplication as repeated addition						C		C	
mental math	G, N	CT, N	C, CC	CT, D, N	C, CC, CT	CT, H	C, CC, N	C, CC	C, CT
estimation	CT		M	CL		C, H	M	N, M	
use calculators			CT		CC	G	CL	CC	CC

Patterns & Functions (Algebra)	Aug/Sept	Oct	Nov	Dec	Jan	Feb	Mar	April	May/June
patterns: sort, classify, and/or order objects	C	M	C, N		C, N	CT, H		C, M	
patterns: recognize, analyze, and/or make predictions	C	C	C	C, N	C	C, H, G, N	C	C	C, N
repeating patterns	C	C	C	C	C	C, G		C	C
growing patterns							C		
symbols: plus, minus, equals	N	N	D, N	N	D, N	N	N	N	N
model addition and subtraction w/ objects	N	N	N	N	N	C, N	N	C, N	N
model multiplication w/ objects			N			C	C	C	
describe qualitative/ quantitative change			N			C, CL	C	C	
algebraic thinking	C, CT, N	C, CT	C, CT	C, CT	C, CT	C, CT, G	C, CT	C, CT	C, CT

KEY

C = CALENDAR   CC = COIN COUNTER   CL = CLOCK
CT = COUNTING TAPE & TEN GRIDS   D = DAILY DEPOSITOR   G = GRAPH
H = ONE HUNDREDTH DAY CELEBRATION   M = MEASUREMENT   N = NUMBER BUILDER

Geometry & Measurement	Aug/Sept	Oct	Nov	Dec	Jan	Feb	Mar	April	May/June
properties of 2-D shapes	C	C	C		C	C		C	G
properties of 3-D shapes			C				M		C, G
spatial relationships: proximity, position, direction	C	C, N	C, N	C, N	C	C, N	C, N	C	C
transformations		C			C			C	C
symmetry/congruence						C		C	
shapes from different perspectives								C	C, G
language of geometry	C	C, M	C	C	C	C	M	C	C, G
geometric shapes in the environment				C	C		M		C, G
length		M	M	D					
capacity/volume						H	M		
weight								M	
yesterday, today, tomorrow	C	C	C	C	C	C	C, CT, G	C	C
names of months	C	C	C	C	C	C	C	C	C
days of week	C	C	C	C	C	C	C	C	C
explore time (analog)	CL	CL	CL	CL	CL	CL	CL		
explore time (digital)	CL	CL	CL	CL	CL	CL	CL		
hours in a day	CL	CL	CL	CL	CL	CL	CL		
minutes in an hour	CL	CL	CL	CL	CL	CL	CL		
money: pennies/nickels			CC	CC	CC	CC	CC	CC	CC
money: dimes				CC	CC	CC	CC	CC	CC
money: quarters						CC	CC	CC	CC
money: dollars								CC	CC
money: mixed coins			CC	CC	CC	CC	CC	CC	CC
make change/choose coins for purchase			CC	CC	CC	CC	CC	CC	CC
temperature		G			G			G	
standard units			M				M		
nonstandard units		M	M				M	M	
measurement tools							M	M	
common benchmarks	CL	CL, M					M	M	
compare measurements		M	M	CL, D	CL	CL	CL	M	
estimate measurements							M	M	

KEY

C = CALENDAR   CC = COIN COUNTER   CL = CLOCK
CT = COUNTING TAPE & TEN GRIDS   D = DAILY DEPOSITOR   G = GRAPH
H = ONE HUNDREDTH DAY CELEBRATION   M = MEASUREMENT   N = NUMBER BUILDER

Data Analysis/Probability	Aug/Sept	Oct	Nov	Dec	Jan	Feb	Mar	April	May/June
gather data		C, G			CL, G	CC, G, H	G, M	G, M	G
organize data		C, G		C	CL, G	CC, CL, G, H	G	C, G, M	G
bar graph		C, G			G	G, H	G	G	G
picture graph	G	G			G	G			
tally charts		CL							
analyze data and make predictions	C, G	C, G		C	G	C, CC	C, G	C, G, M	C, N
sort and classify objects by attributes		C	C					C, M	C, G
describe parts of data set and whole set	G	C, G	C	C	C, G	C, H	C, G	C, M, G	C, G
probability: likelihood and outcomes		C, G			G	CC			

Problem Solving	Aug/Sept	Oct	Nov	Dec	Jan	Feb	Mar	April	May/June
apply a variety of appropriate strategies to solve problems (i.e. guess and check, make a list)	C, G, N	C, CT, N	C, CC, CT	C, CC, CT	CC, CT, D	C, CC, CT, H, N	C, CC, G, M	C, CC, CT, G, M, N	C, CC, N
monitor and reflect on the process of mathematical problem solving	C, G, N	C, CT, N	C, CC, CT, N	C, CC, CT, D, N	CC, CT, D, N	C, CC, CT, H, N	C, CC, G, M, N	C, CT, G, M, N	C, CT, N
choose appropriate computation methods (pencil/paper; estimate; calculator, mental math)	N	N	CC, N	CT, D, N	N	G, H, N	CC, N	N	N

Reasoning & Proof	Aug/Sept	Oct	Nov	Dec	Jan	Feb	Mar	April	May/June
recognize reasoning and proof as fundamental aspects of mathematics	C, G, N	C, CT, G, N	C, CC, CT, D	C, CC, CT, D	C, CC, CT, D	C, CC, CT, G, H, N	C, CC, CT, G, M	C, CT, G, M, N	C, CT, N
select and use various types of reasoning and methods of proof	C, G, N	C, CT, G, N	C, CC, CT, D	C, CC, CT, D	CC, CT, D	C, CC, CT, G, H, N	C, CC, CT, G, M	C, CT, G, M, N	C, CT, N

Communication, Connections & Representation	Aug/Sept	Oct	Nov	Dec	Jan	Feb	Mar	April	May/June
communicate mathematical thinking	C, G, N	C, CT, G, N	C, CC, CT, D, N	C, CC, CT, D, N	CC, CT, D, N	C, CC, CT, G, H, N	C, CC, G, M, N	C, CT, G, M, N	C, CT, N
recognize and use connections among mathematical ideas	C, G, N	C, CT, G, N	C, CC, CT, D	C, CC, CT, D	CC, CT, D	C, CC, CT, G, H, N	C, CC, G, M	C, CT, G, M, N	C, CT, N
use representations to model and interpret mathematical phenomena	C, G, N	C, CT, G, N	C, CC, CT, D	C, CC, CT, D	CC, CT, D	C, CC, CT, G, H, N	C, CC, G, M	C, CT, G, M, N	C, CT, N

Every Day Calendar

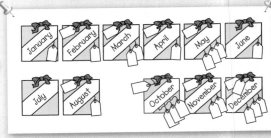

Birthday Data Graph

Clock

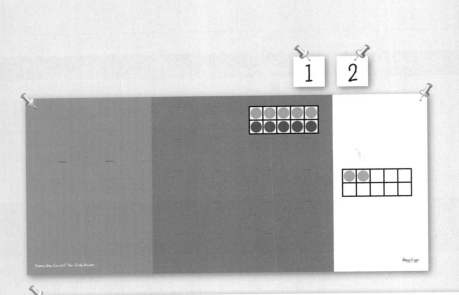

Counting Tape and Ten Grids

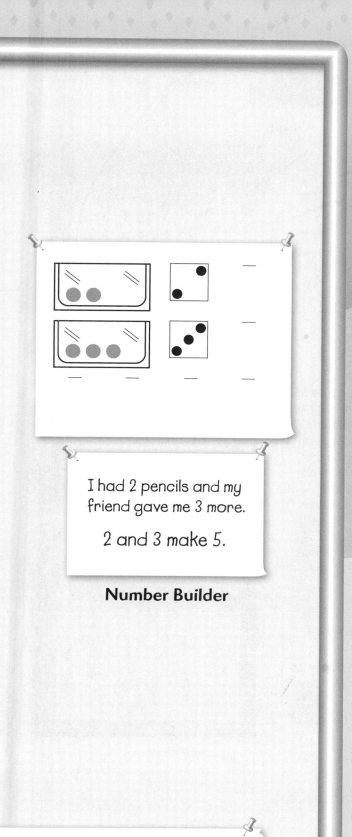

I had 2 pencils and my friend gave me 3 more.

2 and 3 make 5.

Number Builder

AUGUST/SEPTEMBER ELEMENTS

know the days of the week, analyze and predict patterns

see combinations for 5, use language of addition and subtraction, tell addition and subtraction stories, record number sentences

compare and order quantities, group and count by tens, fives, and ones, learn 5+ facts

read the minute hand, count by fives and ones

identify and order months of the year, interpret birthday data, count and compare small quantities

Getting started requires only a few elements of Every Day Counts Calendar Math during the time that establishing classroom routines and getting to know the children are your highest priorities.

Both the Clock and the Counting Tape and Ten Grids use the number of days in school, so there is an advantage to beginning them as soon as possible. If your school year starts in August, begin using them right away. The Counting Tape should be displayed on the first day of school. To acknowledge any August birthdays, you can get started with the Graph.

The Calendar Pieces provided for August are a preview of the September pieces. You may want to allow children simply to observe the Calendar routine in August, and begin discussions in September. If, in September, children can begin to participate in group discussions and begin to develop the language for talking about the Calendar, then they will be able to engage in this activity in more depth in months to come.

Number Builder begins the year reviewing concepts of addition and subtraction and facts for sums of five. Introduce this element early in September.

Number & Operations   Algebra   Geometry   Measurement   Data & Probability
Problem Solving   Reasoning   Communication   Connections   Representation

CALENDAR

Concepts & Skills

- Analyze and predict patterns
- Know the days of the week in order
- Count with one-to-one correspondence
- Match quantities with numerals
- Compare numbers
- Develop number sense

Materials for the Year

Every Day Calendar; Month Strip and Calendar Pieces for the current month; Today Marker; Calendar Record (TR1)

Author Notes

"The Every Day Calendar uses numbered Calendar Pieces that create a specific color and shape pattern as they are attached during the course of the month. Because the Calendar Pieces gradually reveal a pattern, the Calendar provides an invitation to search for connections between the color, shape, and number patterns that appear. "What will be the color of today's date?" encourages children to think. They consider all the accumulated data as they search for a repeating pattern. Early predictions, based on too little data, may be incorrect, which will allow children to see how easy it is to jump to conclusions. As more of the pattern is revealed, children can determine the color of a piece that will appear on any future date using a variety of strategies. At month's end, ask children to describe all the different patterns they see."

Daily Routine

- The first week of September, display the name of the month above the Calendar and help children read it aloud.
- Each day attach the Calendar Piece for that day. (If the month begins on a day without school, catch up to the current date.) On Mondays, add the Calendar Pieces for Saturday and Sunday.
- Attach the Today Marker above the day's name to indicate the day of the week.
- Help the class read the date using the Calendar. For example, "Today is Tuesday, September 8."
- Once a week allow for an extended discussion of the patterns.

DISCUSSION

For the Beginning of the Month

As you introduce the Calendar, take time to ask the children what they notice about the blank Calendar. Discuss the words that appear, count the number of blank spaces in each row, and focus on the different

Ongoing Assessment

1. What will today's piece look like? What number will it have on it?
2. What do you see that keeps happening over and over?
3. How are all of the squares alike?

The September Calendar Pieces create an ABB pattern using one purple circle followed by two green squares.

In August one blue circle was followed by two yellow squares.

color on the ends of each row. Toward the end of the first week, you might ask some of the following questions to focus attention on the Calendar.

Number Sense To focus on number relationships:

- What numbers have we seen so far?
- Would someone like to point out tomorrow's space on the Calendar?
- What number do you think will be on tomorrow's piece?
- How many squares have we put up? How many circles?

Algebraic Thinking To look for similarities and differences:

- How are the pieces we've put up so far the same? (They all have numbers.)
- How are they different? (The colors and shapes change and the numbers are different.)

If some children recognize the possibility of a repeating color pattern at this time, acknowledge the patterns they point out and suggest it will be fun to see if the colors continue in this way. If no mention of a pattern is made, do not point it out at this time. You may want to build the pattern with connecting cubes by adding one cube each day to correspond with the purple, green, green pattern this month. Place it near the Calendar for reference.

> Sample vocabulary words are also defined and illustrated on TR27 and TR28. Encourage children to practice using these terms in class discussions.

For the End of the Second Week
Sample Dialogue

Teacher: Let's look at the Calendar. Today is September 11th. What will tomorrow be?

Class: The 12th.

Teacher: Yes, 11 and 1 more will be 12. What color do you think tomorrow's piece will be?

Child: Green.

Teacher: Who agrees and thinks it will be green? Who thinks it might be a different color? Would someone who thinks it will be green share how you decided this?

Child: There are 2 greens together all the time.

Teacher: Let's see. 2 and 3 are green; 5 and 6 are green; 8 and 9 are green. So you think that green 11 needs a green next to it? That makes sense. Would anyone else who thinks it will be green be willing to share another way you figured this out?

Child: The colors go purple, green, green, purple, green, green, so 12 is going to be green.

Teacher: Two children saw something happening over and over on the Calendar that helped them predict a color for 12. They each saw a pattern. One child saw the greens together over and over. Another saw the purple, green, green pattern happen again and again. When you see a pattern happening over and over, it can often help you predict what will come next. Let's look at tomorrow's piece. Yes, it's green just as many of you predicted.

The activity might be extended to give children another way to experience patterns and their predictability. For example, translate the pattern into body movements. Encourage students to suggest a

"What color do you think tomorrow's piece will be?"

movement to go with purple and another to go with green. Reading the pattern, "purple, green, green" might translate to tap head, legs, legs with your hands. Instead of stopping on 11, continue to point to the blank spaces on the Calendar as children continue saying and acting out the pattern. Try it again with different motions.

For Throughout the Month

These questions might be helpful for discussion throughout the month.

Number Sense To provide experience counting with ordinal and cardinal numbers:

- What will our piece look like in 2 days? In 4 days?
- Let's find the 2nd Monday. What did our piece look like? How about the 3rd Friday?
- How many days have we had so far this week? How many more days until we have had 7 days this week?

Algebraic Thinking, Geometry To search for patterns and describe the attributes of squares (square rectangles):

- What is the same about all of these squares? (Discuss that they have 4 equal sides, 4 square corners, straight sides, and any other observations that may evolve.)
- What things do you see that keep happening over and over?

To Sum Up

At month's end, ask for volunteers to share the different patterns they see happening over and over on the Calendar. Suggestions for interpreting the Calendar pattern in ways other than body movements will be made in upcoming months. By the year's end, children will be recognizing patterns all around them.

HELPFUL HINTS

- Some teachers prefer to make the Calendar Pieces go with the seasons, for example, red schoolhouses and yellow school buses for September. These can add a special touch to the Calendar. Some seasonal calendar shapes are available commercially. Keep them simple so children can see the colors and numbers clearly.
- When patterns appear in places in the environment other than the Calendar, point them out. Invite children to be on the lookout as well.
- You may want to hang a commercial calendar near the bulletin board so the children can make connections between the calendars.

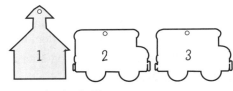

Seasonal Calendar Pieces

NUMBER BUILDER

Concepts & Skills

- Understand processes of addition and subtraction
- Use the language of addition and subtraction
- See part and whole relationships
- Use symbolic notation to record addition and subtraction
- Match quantities and numerals
- Tell number stories relating to addition facts

Ongoing Assessment

1. Tell me a story to go with 3 + 2.
2. Tell us three ways to make 5.
3. What do I need to add to 3 to get to 5?

Materials for the Year

11" × 17" background mat; 12 paper clips; two 3" × 6" clear pockets; 2 sets of 0–9 Domino Halves (TR5); recording paper; counters

Author Notes

"The Number Builder focuses each month on a single quantity for the children to see and talk about. Counters representing that quantity are placed in clear vinyl pockets in different combinations while matching half-Dominoes are hung beside the pockets. The emphasis is on the teacher and children offering addition, subtraction, and comparison stories that go with the sets shown in the two pockets.

September's focus will be on combinations for 5. Other months will consider in turn 6, 7, 8, 9, and 10. Variations occur in January when Number Builder examines "doubles" and "doubles plus one", and in April and May when combinations for 11 through 18 are explored.

The main purpose of Number Builder for the first two weeks of September is to help children discover the process of addition and subtraction featuring the quantity of 5. When the discussions are open-ended and divergent thinking develops, the counters in the pockets may sometimes spark stories that reveal different relationships. It is important to be open to any stories that describe relationships children see. Recording a story with both words and numbers helps children begin to connect their stories to symbolic notation."

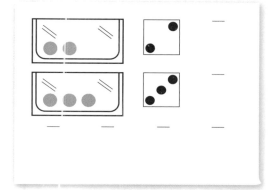

I had 2 pencils and my friend gave me 3 more.

2 and 3 make 5.

Setup

On a horizontal 11" × 17" sheet of heavy plain paper, cut 3 rows of 4 paper clip slits, spaced to hold small clear pockets on the left side and Domino Halves on the right. (See Getting Started, page 8.) On the left side of this mat clip two plastic pockets, one above the other. On the right side, tape on paper clips to hold the Domino Halves. Hang recording paper near the mat.

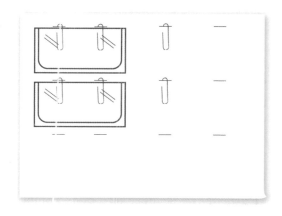

Daily Routine

- Two or three days a week, invite a child to distribute five counters between the two pockets.
- Clip matching Domino Halves next to the pockets.
- Have volunteers tell addition, subtraction, or comparison stories to match the counter arrangement. Record one story and the corresponding number sentence. Other stories can be represented by the number sentence alone.
- Explore other combinations for 5 as time allows, and encourage children to tell stories.
- After two weeks, empty the mat and play *Make the Sum*. (See Discussion for Later in the Month.)

DISCUSSION

For the First Two Weeks

Initially, the majority of stories will likely focus around addition, but be open to any story corresponding to the counters. If 3 counters are in the top pocket and 2 are below, one child's story might be, "I found 3 rocks last week and 2 this week. So now I have 5."

Record a paraphrased version of the story in words on the record sheet along with a symbolic number sentence, in this case, 3 + 2 = 5. Help the class read the number sentence back using everyday language. Linking everyday words that children readily understand to the math notation helps them see that symbolic math is nothing mysterious. Formal math terms can be used interchangeably with everyday language as the year goes on so children pick up their meanings over time. A brief discussion such as the following might occur in your classroom.

Sample Dialogue

Teacher: What is our special number for this month?

Class: 5.

Teacher: Here are 5 counters. Who can show us one way to make 5?

Child: We could put 3 in the top pocket and 2 in the bottom pocket.

Teacher: Okay, while you do that, I will also put up the Dominoes to show 3 and 2. Let's all think of a story to match our counters.

Child: I know a story. I had 3 cats and I found 2 more. Now I have 5 cats.

Teacher: Does this story match our counters?

Class: Yes.

Teacher: I have written this story with words. Now how do we show it with numbers? (Accept suggestions for connecting the story to numbers. You may initially record *3 and 2 make 5*, or the number sentence *3 + 2 = 5*.)

Teacher: Who has another story to share?

Child: I had 3 pennies and my mom gave me 2 more.

Teacher: These are good stories. (Empty the pockets.) Is there another way that we could show 5?

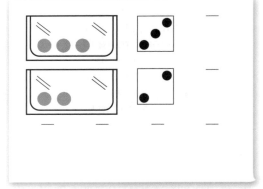

I had 3 cookies and my mom gave me 2 more.

3 + 2 = 5

Child: We could put 1 in the top pocket and 4 in the bottom pocket and I have a story for this. I had 1 pumpkin and then I got 4 more.

Teacher: Does this story match our counters? How could we show this with numbers?

You may also want to model some subtraction stories where counters from one pocket and the adjacent Domino are removed.

For Later in the Month

Around the third week of the month remove everything from the background mat so only the clips are remaining. Two or three days a week, randomly clip two sets of 0 through 5 Dominoes face up on the background mat to play *Make the Sum*.

Ask for volunteers to select one or two Dominoes with a sum of 5. For example one child might select the Domino for 4 and the Domino for 1. After stating the number sentence *4 and 1 make 5*, these two cards are removed and another child takes a turn. Record each number sentence as it is stated. Continue until all cards are removed.

On the last day that *Make a Sum* is played, mount the Domino Halves totalling 5 on heavy paper or TR6 to create permanent Domino Cards. Keep these on a ring together for review in future months.

HELPFUL HINTS

- Using a variety of objects in place of counters will provide a range of storytelling situations for children to respond to. Suggestions include buttons, small rocks, bread tags, or milk caps, which children can bring from home.

- You may find it helpful to remove the 5 counters from the pockets and let children use them to act out their stories, placing them into the pockets as they talk.

- If you record the stories on paper, they can be collected into booklets and kept in the classroom library for future browsing. Some teachers who have recorded the number sentences at the bottom of each sheet create a "flip and match book" by cutting the number sentences off the sheet, mixing up their order, and then stapling both the stories and the number sentences into a new booklet. Children can then flip through the book together and connect the stories to their matching number sentences.

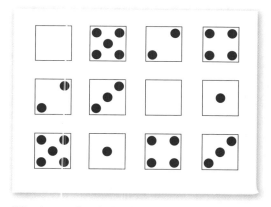

"I'll take the 0 and the 5 in the top row."

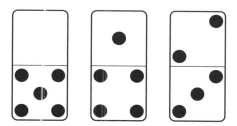

Make permanent Domino Cards for 5 to use for review.

COUNTING TAPE AND TEN GRIDS

Concepts & Skills

- Develop number sense and see number patterns
- Count with one-to-one correspondence
- Group and count by tens, fives, and ones
- Understand teen numbers and place value
- Match quantities with numerals
- Compare and order quantities
- Count one more and one less
- See part/part/whole combinations for 5 and 10
- Use mental math for adding and subtracting ten

Materials for the Year

Adding machine tape; 200 three-inch squares (20 each of 10 different colors); glue stick; 20 yellow dot stickers (optional); Ten Grids Poster; 20 Ten Grids (TR9); a blue and a red felt pen or blue and red $\frac{3}{4}$" dot stickers (100 of each); sticky notes or 0–9 Digit Cards (TR10) on rings

The Counting Tape is a time line for recording each day of first grade.

Author Notes

"The Counting Tape is a time line for recording each day of first grade. As children see a new square added to the Counting Tape each day and see the number for that school day recorded, they will become more familiar with increasing quantities and the numbers that represent them.

Every 10 days the color of the squares changes, helping children to see the patterns from decade to decade. As they count the shapes each day, they practice the counting sequence. They also count the groups of ten and the extra ones to develop an understanding of place value. From the 101st day on, children see the pattern of the first 99 days repeated.

The Counting Tape reveals other relationships as well. Its linearity assists children in making comparisons. For example, they can see that a row of 20 is twice as long as a row of 10 and it is easy to see which is more, 12 or 21. Making many such comparisons fosters children's development of number sense. For this reason find a place for the Counting Tape where it can extend as far as possible without a break.

The accompanying Ten Grids provide a simultaneous pictorial representation of the number of school days. Every 10 days a Ten Grid is filled and moved to the tens place. As children see the tens digit change each time this happens, they can gradually construct an understanding of our base ten numeration system. On the one hundredth day of school, they are exposed to the idea of 10 tens making 100. They learn to count by hundreds, tens, and ones and to read and write numbers, knowing what the digits represent.

The Ten Grids are also a powerful visual model to help children see combinations for five and for ten. The dots are organized to help children think of the numbers 6, 7, 8, 9, and 10 as 5 + 1, 5 + 2, 5 + 3, 5 + 4, and 5 + 5. This can lead to "pulling out fives" to make ten as a strategy when joining sets of six, seven, eight, and nine.

The Ten Grids also provides experience with counting by tens and ones, by fives and ones, and by tens, fives, and ones—skills children need when reading a clock, adding coins, grouping and counting objects, and adding and subtracting numbers greater than 10."

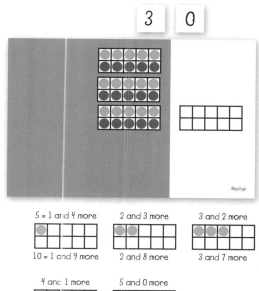

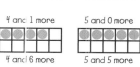

Daily Routine

Counting Tape

- Attach one square to the Counting Tape each school day beginning with the first day of school.

- Use squares that are all the same color for the first 10 days, then use a different color for the next 10, and so on for each decade to 100.

- This first month, ask the class to count by ones to the day's number. Then count by tens and ones, clapping on the last multiple of ten as a reminder for everyone to begin counting by ones. For example, on the 16th day of school, children count "10 (with a clap), 11, 12, 13, 14, 15, 16."

- After counting the squares, discuss how to write the day's number, saying the number of tens and ones. For example, on the 16th day have the class say with you, "one group of ten" as you point to the 1 in the tens place, and then say, "six extra ones" as you point to the 6 in the ones place.

"Let's count together, 10 (clap!), 11, 12, 13, 14, 15, 16; 1 group of ten and 6 extra ones."

Ten Grids

- Each day of school beginning on the first day of school place one dot sticker or color one dot on a Ten Grid attached to the ones place on the Ten Grid poster.

- Fill the top row first, using blue dots, then fill the bottom row with red dots.

- When a Ten Grid becomes full, move it to the tens place and attach a new, empty grid to the ones place.

- Each day record the number of tens and ones below (or above) each place.

- Have the class count by tens and ones and tell how many dots there are in all. On the 16th day of school, the class would count, "10 (clap!), 11, 12, 13, 14, 15, 16; 1 full ten and 6 ones."

DISCUSSION

For the First Day

As soon as possible, introduce the Counting Tape and Ten Grids. Explain to children that there will be one square and one dot for each day they come to school this year. Ask them to call out the number for you to write on each square, beginning with 1 for Day 1. You might ask them how far around the room they think the Counting Tape will stretch by the 100th day of school.

1

For Later in the Month

Once or twice a week, in addition to the counting and recording activities, engage children in considering other questions. These questions can encourage children to see many relationships and help them construct a variety of number concepts. The list of possibilities is long in order to provide a broad range of questions that can be adapted for use on any school day.

Comparing, Ordering Some questions to develop number sense and vocabulary for comparing and ordering quantities:

- Which is more, 9 squares or 13 squares?
- What day of school came just after Day 6?
- What day of school came just before Day 12?
- What day of school came just after Day 7 and just before Day 9?

Place Value Some questions to foster understanding of place value:

- How many groups of ten do we have so far? How many extras?
- Do we write the groups of ten first or the ones first?
- How many squares would we have if we took off a whole group of ten?

Addition and Subtraction Concepts Some questions to encourage an understanding of one more/one less and two more/two less:

- What day of school will it be in one more day? In two more days?
- What number is one more than today's number? Two more?
- If we added one dot to our Ten Grid, how many dots would we have? What if we added two dots?
- If we took off the last square on our Tape, how many squares would we have? What if we took off two squares?

Algebraic Thinking Some questions to encourage sorting and searching for patterns:

- How many more days until the color will change? How do you know?
- How many days until we have another Ten Grid filled? How do you know?
- How are the squares that come after 10 like the first 10 squares? How are they different?

Number Sense, Mental Math On the 11th through the 19th day of school, ask children if they think the numeral 1 recorded for the tens place means 1 full Ten Grid or 1 dot. As you record each teen number have the class say "one group of ten" as you record the 1 and then say the number of extras as you record the second digit.

Some days focus discussion questions on the not-yet full grid on the ones section.

- How many more dots are needed to get to 5?
- How many to get to a full 10?

After the 10th day you might model taking a full ten off or adding a full ten to the tens section. Children will be able to consider questions such as:

- How many will we have if I take off a full Ten Grid?
- Today we have 13, or one ten and 3 leftover ones. How many more dots do we need to get to 15?

The purpose of asking such questions is to foster children's thinking. Understanding how children arrive at their answers—the processes and strategies they use—is more important than the correct or incorrect responses they may give. By frequently asking, "Would someone be willing to share how you got your answer?" we help children focus on their thinking.

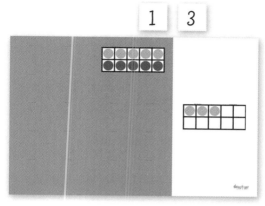

"1 full ten and 3 extras are 13."

HELPFUL HINTS

- If your school year begins in August, begin using the Counting Tape and Ten Grids the first week.
- Adding a yellow dot sticker to the center of the zero in the numerals 10, 20, 30, and so on, helps to make the tens stand out. Some teachers draw on a face and name zero "Zero the Hero." Children greet its appearance with a special song.
- If your school has die-cut shapes available, you may want to substitute other cutouts to create discrete shapes for counting. You can also turn squares on end to make them easier to count.
- The tens and ones record can be done in a variety of ways. Some teachers put up pads of paper and simply tear off the last day's record sheet each day. Others use a clear pocket so the digits can be wiped off and rewritten with an overhead pen each day. Yet another way is to use a set of 0–9 Digit Cards (TR10) in pockets or on rings under each place. Volunteers can change the cards to show each day's new total.
- Some teachers enlarge their Ten Grids so a variety of commercial stickers can be used.

Zero the Hero

Zero the Hero is so cool,
Zero the Hero comes to school!
Zero the Hero saves a space,
So all the other numbers
Will stay in their place!

Sing *Zero the Hero* to the tune of *Three Little Fishies* (*Itty Bitty Pool*).

Number & Operations   Algebra   Geometry   Measurement   Data & Probability
Problem Solving   Reasoning   Communication   Connections   Representation

CLOCK

Concepts & Skills

- Experience duration
- Understand analog and digital clocks
- Learn how many minutes in an hour
- Count by fives and ones
- Read the minute hand

Materials for the Year

Clock cardstock or a copy of the Clock (TR12) with minute hand attached; 9" × 12" clear pocket; blue and red markers with erasable ink

Author Notes

"For the first 60 days of school, the Clock on the bulletin board will have only a minute hand, which moves forward one minute per school day. Thus children get daily experience counting the minutes by fives and ones and reading the minute hand. Once January comes, the routine changes and an hour hand is added to follow the day's date. Both hour and minute hands will move to show one hour passing for each day of the month. In February, the clock will move forward by just a half hour daily. Beginning in March, hour and minute hands are considered together.

Throughout the year, the digital notation is used to help children gain confidence in reading both kinds of clocks. Occasional duration experiments give children the chance to estimate and experience how long a second or a minute is."

Setup

Slide the Clock in to the clear pocket, then attach the minute hand with a paper fastener.

Daily Routine

- Beginning on the first day of school, move the minute hand on the Clock ahead one minute each school day. At the same time, color in one space along the circumference. Alternate between blue and red every 5 days.
- On the fifth day of school, write a 1 just inside the first 5-minute mark to represent one group of 5. On the 10th day of school, write a 2 for two groups of 5, and so on.
- Each day read the position of the minute hand, counting by ones first, and then again by fives and ones, clapping on the last 5 to signal the change to counting by ones. For example, on the 16th day, count the minutes saying "5, 10, 15 (clap), 16!"
- Finally, record the minutes shown by the minute hand, using the digital clock below the clock face. This number should agree with the Counting Tape, which also reflects the days of school.
- Update daily and discuss two or three times a week.

First day of school

DISCUSSION

For the First Day

Sample Dialogue

Teacher: (showing the Every Day Clock to the class) Look around the room. Can you find something that looks a little like this picture?

Child: The clock.

Teacher: Yes, this picture is a lot like our clock. It is round and it has the same marks going around the edge. How is this picture different from the classroom clock?

Child: The picture doesn't have any numbers on it.

Child: The picture just has one hand on it. Our clock has two hands.

Teacher: Good observations. Look at the classroom clock right now. The short hour hand tells us it is just a little after 9:00. The long minute hand pointed straight up when it was 9:00, but now it has moved to the 10th tiny minute mark, so the time is 9:10 or 10 minutes after 9. To help us learn how to read the minute hand, we're going to move the long minute hand on our bulletin board Clock ahead one minute each day we come to school. If we begin straight up at zero and today is the first day of school, which minute mark shall we point it toward today?

For Later in the Month

At least twice a week, after counting the minutes, talk about how many groups of five have passed. Ask children to predict how they will read the minute hand when it reaches the next 5-minute mark. How many more days will it take to get there?

You might designate some days for noticing when the minute hand on the classroom clock matches the position of the minute hand on the Clock. Children can raise their hands when they notice these special times during the day. Take a moment to read the classroom clock, helping children read the hour hand first and then having them read the minutes.

HELPFUL HINTS

- If your school year begins in August, begin using the Clock the first week.

- Some teachers find it helpful to write 5, 10, 15, and so on around the outside of the Clock to help children count by fives.

- The digital notation of minutes can be wiped off and rewritten each day. Some teachers prefer to replace this record with pockets holding number cards. Still others like to use sticky notes to replace the digits daily. The digits can be changed each day to tell the time shown on the Clock.

- With the emphasis on minutes and reading minutes past the hour on the Clock, it would be helpful for children to have a sense of how long one minute is. Ask them to rest their heads on their arms and observe one minute of quiet.

- We have chosen to use the terms *long* and *short* instead of *big* and *little* when referring to the minute and hour hands.

- Bringing in a digital clock may speed up some children's clock-reading skills since they can compare the digits to the positions of the hands on the classroom clock. At home, both types of clocks are rarely in the same room, making such comparisons difficult.

- Although the Every Day Clock is used through December to emphasize the minute hand, it is suggested that the classroom clock or a geared demonstration clock be used simultaneously throughout these months as an aid in reading the hour and minutes together.

Comparing two different clocks

| Number & Operations | Algebra | Geometry | Measurement | Data & Probability |
| Problem Solving | Reasoning | Communication | Connections | Representation |

GRAPH

Concepts & Skills

- Count with one-to-one correspondence
- Read, compare, and order numbers to 30
- Solve problems and use mental math
- Know the months of the year in order
- Interpret organized data

Ongoing Assessment

1. What is this month?
2. Can you name another month?
3. What month is your birthday?

Materials for the Month

Twelve Birthday Packages (TR14); a Gift Tag (TR14) for each child

Author Notes

"Displaying the month's Birthday Package with the gift tags attached guarantees that a child's birthday will not slip past without special recognition. The tags with the names and birthdays on them provide a fun focus for comparing numbers and determining how many days until each upcoming birthday. For the remainder of the year birthday data will be considered during Calendar discussion time."

Setup

Label 12 Birthday Packages with the names of the months. Prepare a Gift Tag for each child, marking it with their name and birth date. Attach them to the appropriate Packages. Display the 12 packages where they can be seen and discussed.

Daily Routine

- On the first day of school, have the month's Birthday Package with the attached tags placed near the Calendar.
- The first week of school invite children to help you read the names of the children whose tags are on the Package. Take the tags from the Package temporarily to mark the birthdays on the Calendar.
- After each birthday has passed return the tag to its Package.
- Update monthly. Discuss at the beginning of each month and on each child's birthday.

DISCUSSION

For the Beginning of the Month

Analyzing Data The tags on the Birthday Package offer experiences in counting with one-to-one correspondence and ordering numbers. The following sample questions are intended to encourage this as children solve the problem of identifying the birthdays on this month's calendar.

- How many children have birthdays this month?
- What do you think the number on each tag means?
- If the number written on each tag is the birthday, which is the first birthday this month and whose is it?
- Whose birthday comes last this month?
- If we put the tags on the Calendar to mark each birthday, which space will get the first birthday of the month? Can you point to it? There is no number in that space, so how did you decide it should go there?
- Where will the next birthday be on the Calendar? Whose birthday is it?

Continue this process until all birthdays for the month have been identified on the Calendar.

For Later in the Month

As the month goes along, you might occasionally ask children to determine how many days it will be until the next birthday. Then ask for volunteers to share how they got their answers. Some will count the spaces on the Calendar. Some will count on their fingers. Others may mentally compute a difference between the birthday and the present date.

With each passing birthday, when asked how many birthdays have come up so far in the month and how many are still to come, children have a chance to look at a different addition combination.

HELPFUL HINTS

- Many summer-birthday children experience disappointment when they are unable to celebrate their birthday with the class. It is, therefore, nice to choose an "unbirthday" for each of these children, perhaps six months before the real birthday on the same day of the month.

- Opening a real birthday package would get a child's birthday off to a great start. It might contain cards from classmates and a special birthday crown, necklace, or badge, adorned with the child's name, to wear for the day.

- If space near the bulletin board is a problem, many teachers like to hang their Birthday Packages on the door of a closet, or on another bulletin board. Each month's Package (and its "unbirthday" if applicable) are always placed on the Calendar board for children to talk about during that month and returned at the month's end.

- Some teachers like to color their Birthday Packages with seasonal colors: white for winter, green for spring, yellow for summer and orange for fall.

Mark children's birthdays on the Calendar with the Package tags.

OCTOBER

Every Day Calendar

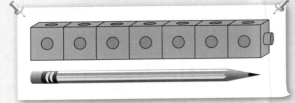

Birthday Data

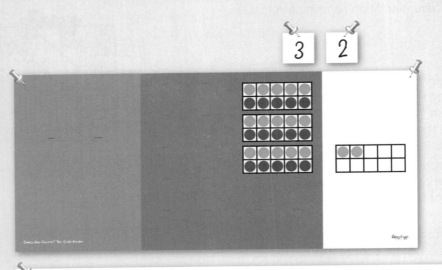

Measurement

Clock

Counting Tape and Ten Grids

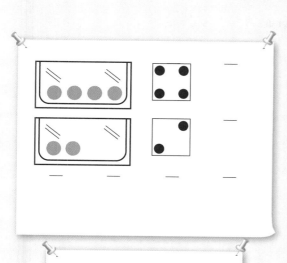

Number Builder

Six kids were playing in the park and 2 went home. How many kids were still playing?

$6 - 2 = 4$

Number Builder

October Morning Weather Sample

	sunny	☀	☀	☀	☀	☀	☀
partly cloudy						
cloudy	☁	☁	☁	☁		
rainy	☂	☂	☂			
snowy						

Graph

OCTOBER ELEMENTS

The Calendar Math elements that were introduced in September will be in use again. The Counting Tape and Ten Grids and the Clock will continue to reflect the number of school days. The Calendar will present a new pattern and include discussion of birthday data. The Graph this month will display a sample of the season's autumn weather. A new element, Measurement, will appear this month to give children frequent opportunities to estimate and compare the lengths of an assortment of classroom objects using nonstandard units.

CALENDAR

Concepts & Skills

- Know the months of the year in order
- Count, compare, and order small quantities
- Recognize, analyze, and predict patterns
- Know the days of the week in order
- Count with one-to-one correspondence
- Match quantities with numerals
- Identify the attributes of a rectangle
- Solve problems

Author Notes

"This month's pattern will allow many interpretations depending on the background of your children. An upright rectangle, the same rectangle lying down, and a square rectangle will represent the rectangles. (The square is a special rectangle. At times, we will refer to the square as a square rectangle. You can determine the language that is most appropriate for your children.) Providing a variety of rectangles gives children opportunities to move beyond the common representation of a four-sided figure with two horizontal long sides, and to make generalizations about rectangles. Some children will simply refer to this pattern as a red, red, red, yellow pattern. Others may notice the different rectangles and use them in their description of the pattern.

This month *Draw and Replace,* a probability game played throughout the month, will also be featured in the Helpful Hints."

Daily Routine

- At the beginning of the month ask the class to find the October Birthday Package, and place it near the Calendar.
- Have the class find where on the Calendar to place the individual tags.
- Continue to update the Calendar daily.
- Once a week allow time for the children to share their observations and to interpret the month's pattern.

DISCUSSION

For the Beginning of the Month

Before you discuss the array of Birthday Packages, many children will have already found their names and noticed whether their package has only a few or many other tags. The following are examples of the kinds of questions that draw on children's observations and foster counting and comparing.

- How many names are on your birthday month's package?
- Which Birthday Package has the most names on it?

Ongoing Assessment

1. What is the name of this month?
2. What will our Calendar piece look like in 2 days? In 4 days?
3. Have we had more squares or more circles? Convince us.

The October Calendar Pieces use red circles and yellow rectangles to create an AAAB pattern in the order red circle, red circle, red circle, yellow rectangle. The rectangles include special square rectangles.

- Are there any months with no birthdays? Just 1 birthday?
- Can you find some packages with the same number of tags?
- If January is month one, and the next month, February, is month two, what month is October?

Discussion

For After the Second Week

Some questions that tend to encourage observations and sharing thoughts about the new pattern that is appearing might include the following.

Algebraic Thinking To search for patterns:

- Today is Tuesday, October __. So what will tomorrow be?
- What color do you think tomorrow's piece will be?
- How did you figure this out? What helped you to know it would be this color?
- Could someone share a different way that helped them?
- Is this a pattern? Convince us.

Geometry To discover the attributes of rectangles :

- How are the yellow shapes alike? How are they different?
- Do they all have "square corners," corners that go "straight up and straight out" or look like a capital "L"?
- Are the sides curved or straight?

To help children broaden their concept of pattern beyond the Calendar, have them occasionally interpret the month's AAAB color pattern using body motions. By letting the motion pattern continue on its own momentum after the Calendar Pieces run out, children can feel the strong predictability of pattern. Encourage children to suggest and try out two or three different interpretations of the pattern within a session. In addition to translating the pattern into body movements, continue to involve children in creating a pattern "train" to copy and extend the month's color pattern using materials available in the room.

For the End of the Month

To wrap up the month's discussion of patterns, ask children to communicate some of the things they have noticed about the Calendar this month.

Helpful Hints

- When new children enter the classroom later in the year, be sure to add tags to the appropriate Birthday Package for them.
- Don't worry about those who aren't picking up the idea of pattern at this time. Month after month of experiencing patterns and listening to the observations of their "pattern-seeing" peers will help them. Ignore the stomps that should have been claps. By asking everyone to make predictions, but asking only for volunteers to share their reasoning, each child will begin to see patterns. The ranks of volunteers will expand with each passing week.

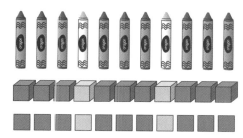

October Pattern Trains

"The pattern is red, red, red, yellow."

"The yellows go down like stairs."

"The rectangles change but they go in a pattern too."

- You may want to introduce *Draw and Replace* as a probability activity this month. It will provide the children with opportunities to make predictions regarding the likelihood of outcomes. Show the children the 4 unnumbered Calendar Pieces from the October Calendar (three red and one yellow) and then place the pieces in a small paper sack. Have children predict which piece will be the most likely to be pulled from the bag and what the final results might look like. Record their predictions on paper.

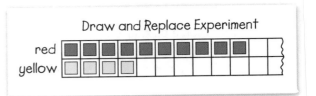

Draw and Replace Experiment

- One day each week, draw and replace one Calendar Piece 15 times for a total of 60 draws over the course of the month.

- Use a red crayon for circles and a yellow crayon for the rectangles to color one square on a long strip of one-inch graph paper for each draw. Or collect a red or yellow connecting cube for each draw.

- **Analyzing Data** Discuss the predictions and the results to encourage thinking about probability:

  - Which color has more so far?

  - Is it likely at the end of the month that red will have more or that yellow will have more? Is there a chance that they will be the same?

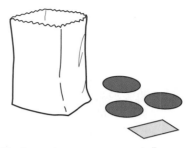

"So far we have way more reds."

Number & Operations		Algebra		Geometry		Measurement		Data & Probability	
	Problem Solving		Reasoning		Communication		Connections		Representation

NUMBER BUILDER

Concepts & Skills

- Understand processes of addition and subtraction
- Use the language of addition and subtraction
- Discuss part and whole relationships for 6
- Use symbolic notation to record addition and subtraction
- Match quantities and numerals
- Share number stories describing the different relationships represented by the counters

Ongoing Assessment

1. How can we "break 6 apart"?
2. Which number is greater, 4 or 2? Why?
3. Can you tell me a take away story for 6, where one of the parts is taken away?

Daily Routine

- During the first two weeks of this month, allow a volunteer to count out 6 counters and choose how to place them into the two pockets. Encourage children to break up the group in new ways, so that after 2 weeks the class has seen 6 and 0, 5 and 1, 4 and 2, and 3 and 3 several times.

- Clip matching Domino Halves to the right of the pockets to show the same sum.

- Have children share stories to correspond to the numbers of counters. Record some of the stories for the class to read later.

- The last two weeks, play *Make the Sum* or *Make a Match*. (See Discussion.)

DISCUSSION

For the First Two Weeks of the Month

Below are some questions that you might ask to elicit a discussion about the processes of addition, subtraction, and comparison, as well as to explore the combinations for 6.

- Looking at the 4 and 2 we have represented, who has a story where we add or combine all of the counters?
- What do we do when we `add`?
- Looking at our whole amount of 6, who has a take away story where one part of our 6 is taken away?
- We wrote 6 − 2 = 4 to describe our story with numbers. Where did the 6 come from? What does the 4 tell us?
- How many different ways can we "break 6 apart"?
- If we put 4 counters in the top pocket, how many more would we need in the bottom pocket to make a total of 6?
- Is 4 + 2 the same as 6?
- Which is `greater`, the top pocket with 4 or the bottom pocket with 2? How many more are in the top pocket?

Since many children will be comfortable with telling addition stories, you may want to take the opportunity to invite and model more "take away" stories this month.

Six kids were playing in the park and 2 went home. How many kids were still playing?
6 − 2 = 4

For the Third Week

Around the third week of the month, sort out a set of 0 through 6 Domino Halves to play a variation on *Make the Sum*. Holding the Domino Halves facedown, invite a child to draw one. Have the child place this quantity of counters in the top pocket and clip the Domino adjacent to the pocket. If a 4 has been drawn, 4 counters would be placed in the pocket and the Domino for 4 hung beside it. Continue to have individual children draw a Domino from you until the addend that will make a total of 6 is drawn. This is another version of *Make the Sum* played in September. Your discussion might evolve like this one:

Teacher: Since the Domino for 4 was drawn, we hung it up and put 4 counters in the pocket. Think about what we need to add to 4 to make 6. Who would like to continue our search by drawing another card?

Child: I drew a 3.

Teacher: Will this work for us? Let's count on from 4 to see what 4 + 3 will equal.

Class: 4, 5, 6, 7.

Teacher: Will this work?

Child: No, 3 and 4 make 7.

Teacher: We need another person to draw.

Child: I drew a 1. This won't work because 4 and 1 is 5.

Teacher: Let's draw again.

Child: I got a 2. Yes, 4 and 2 make 6. This will work. (The child places 2 counters in the bottom pocket and hangs up the Domino for 2.) **MORE ▶**

Teacher: Let's write this combination on our record sheet. Are we finished for today or should we try another search?

Class: Another search!

Teacher: Let's take down the Dominoes and empty the pockets. Who is ready to draw the first card?

For the Fourth Week

Around the fourth week of the month remove everything but the clips from the background mat. Randomly clip two sets of 1 through 5 Dominoes facedown on the background to play the *Make a Match* memory game.

Ask for volunteers to select 2 Dominoes to turn over. If the Dominoes combine to make 6, they are removed. If not, they are turned facedown in their original places. Volunteers continue to draw until all possible sums for 6 have been made. When a sum for 6 is made, the number sentence is stated and the teacher records it.

On the last day that *Make a Match* is played, mount the pairs of Domino Halves totaling 6 on TR6 to create a Domino Card. These can be kept on a ring for review in future months.

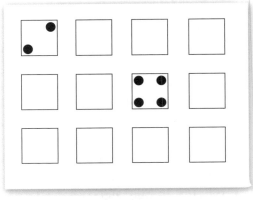

"2 and 4 make 6 so I can take these cards."

HELPFUL HINT

• *Make the Sum* can be played for independent practice using 0–6 Ten Grid Number Cards (TR8). Place cards facedown in a stack. Players take turns drawing a card and placing it faceup in a line. Upon drawing a card the player searches the shared lineup of cards and takes any cards with a sum of 6. The player must state the sum before taking the cards. The player with the most cards at the end of play wins.

Number & Operations	Algebra	Geometry	Measurement	Data & Probability
Problem Solving	Reasoning	Communication	Connections	Representation

MEASUREMENT

Concepts & Skills

• Estimate lengths and compare lengths
• Order lengths
• Use the language of *longer, shorter, same length*
• Measure lengths with nonstandard units

Ongoing Assessment

1. Show me something shorter than this pencil.
2. Which is longer, _____ or _____?
3. Which is shorter, _____ or _____?

Materials for October

Manipulatives such as connecting cubes and links; classroom items such as a stapler, an eraser, a paintbrush, a craft stick, a piece of yarn, a shoe

Author Notes

"When learning about measurement children need to be exposed to the idea of the length of an object. Then children can begin to compare lengths using vocabulary such as *longer, shorter, the same length as*, etc. Thereafter, children are ready to compare the length of objects with nonstandard measures and finally with standard measures. You may want to allow children to compare and measure at centers after this month of introducing the concept to them. This month you may want to make a point of using the words *longer, shorter,* and *the same length as* in appropriate contexts throughout the day."

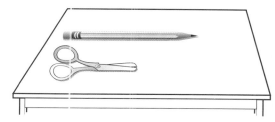

"The pencil is longer than the scissors."

Daily Routine

- **The first two weeks** choose two objects from the collection and lay them out skewed so that the children cannot tell immediately whether or not the objects are the same length.

- Ask the children which object they think is longer. Let them make a prediction and then carefully model how to line up the ends of the objects so that they can tell which is longer.

- Use comparison words *longer, shorter,* or *the same length as* to describe the relative lengths. For example, "The paintbrush is longer than the marker."

- **The third week** have children practice lining up three or more objects in order of length.

- **The last week** have children first estimate how long an object is in a nonstandard unit and then measure it.

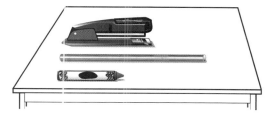

"Can you put these in order from shortest to longest?"

DISCUSSION

For the Third Week

Comparing This week pull out three objects to compare their length. You might want to ask some of the following questions:

- Which one do you think is longer?
- How can we tell for sure?
- Which one is shorter?
- Are any of these objects the same length or of equal length?

Ordering The following questions use the language of ordering:

- How do we line up the objects by length?
- Which is the longest?
- Which object is the shortest?
- Which object is in between?

Model for the children statements that order the length of three objects. For example, "The crayon is shorter than the pencil which is shorter than the ruler, which is the longest," or "The ruler is longer than the pencil which is longer than the crayon, which is the shortest of all."

For the Fourth Week

The following discussion to guide children in using nonstandard units of length might occur in your classroom.

Sample Dialogue

Teacher: I have taken out a pencil and some connecting cubes. Who can tell me how many connecting cubes it will take to make a line as long as the pencil?

Child: Seven.

Child: More than 10.

Teacher: Good estimating! I am going to put the connecting cube at the very end of the pencil.

Teacher: Snap seven cubes on here. Is that as long as the pencil?

Child: We need more.

Teacher: Let's put on four more.

Child: Now we have 11 cubes but it is still too short.

Child: I think we need two more. That will be 13.

Teacher: Do you agree class? Do you think two more will make the stack of connecting cubes as long as the pencil? Will they both be the same length?

"Is the pencil the same length as the connecting cubes?"

HELPFUL HINT

- Many teachers like to compare the heights of children by making an inch paper strip (TR17) as tall as each child. The teacher hangs two of them up and asks, "Which is taller, Lucy's strip or Benjamiah's strip?" Then some teachers hang all of the strips up in order.

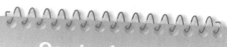

Number & Operations	Algebra	Geometry	Measurement	Data & Probability
Problem Solving	Reasoning	Communication	Connections	Representation

COUNTING TAPE AND TEN GRIDS

Concepts & Skills

- Develop number sense
- Count with one-to-one correspondence
- Group and count by tens, fives, and ones
- Understand place value
- Compare and order quantities
- Count on and count back
- See number patterns
- See 6, 7, 8, 9 as 5 plus more
- Add or subtract 10
- Use the language of duration
- Solve problems

Ongoing Assessment

1. How many squares are on the Counting Tape today?

2. How many groups of ten squares do we see? How many full Ten Grids do we have?

3. What number is just after today's number?

Daily Routine

- Each school day continue to add a square to the Counting Tape. Count by tens and ones to the day's number.

- Continue to add a new dot each school day to the Ten Grids, filling the top row first with blue dots and the second row with red dots. Continue to move a Grid to the tens place when it is filled.

- Count the dots by tens, fives, and ones as appropriate. For example, on the 29th day of school the class would count, "10, 20, 25, 26, 27, 28, 29."

- Have the class focus on each element alone and both together as they consider questions about adding and subtracting 10, comparing numbers and quantities, finding how many more, and matching quantities to numerals.

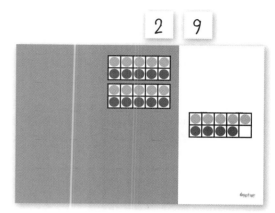

"I can prove it. 10 and 10 is 20 and 9 more is 29."

"Me too. 5, 10, 15, 20, 25, 26, 27, 28, 29."

DISCUSSION

For During the Month

Continue comparing, counting on, counting back, and counting by tens and one as you adapt many of the September questions to the larger numbers now appearing on the Counting Tape and on the Ten Grids.

Ordering, Comparing, Mental Math Encourage children to use either the Counting Tape or the Ten Grids to answer questions to develop mental math skills and number sense, ordering numbers and comparing quantities, and counting on and counting back.

- We have 28 dots today. How many did we have ten days ago?

- How many will we have tomorrow?

- How many more dots do we need to get another full ten?

- How many dots until we have 30?

- How many dots will be left on this Ten Grid if we take away all the red ones? All the blue ones?

- Which came first, Day 13 or Day 15? What number is less, 13 or 15?

- What day of school came just after Day 3? Day 13? Day 23?

- What number is one more than 4? 14? 24? What number is one less than 4? 14? 24?

- What day of school came just before Day 5? Day 15? Day 25?

- What day came between Day 11 and Day 13?

- (on Day 25) How many blue dots would we take away to go back to 24? To 23?

- (again on Day 25) How many red dots will we have on day 26? Day 27?

- How many more is 25 than 24? Than 23?

- How many more days must we come to school to get up to the 30th day? How many more red dots do we need?

- How many more dots until we fill another Ten Grid?

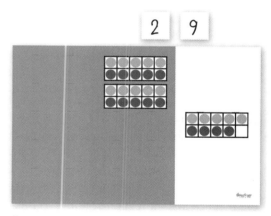

"How many dots until we have 30?"

Place Value Questions to foster place value understanding:

- How many dots would we have if we took away one full Ten Grid?
- How many squares would we have on the Counting Tape if we took off the first group of ten?

Patterns Questions that encourage sorting and the search for patterns:

- How many more days until the color on the Counting Tape will change again?
- How are the squares in the twenties like the squares up to 10?

Continue to ask children to share how they are arriving at their answers. Toward the end of the month, ask children to estimate how far they think the Counting Tape squares will stretch by the hundredth day of school. If they made an earlier guess in September, ask them to compare it with their present estimates to see if they are the same or different.

HELPFUL HINTS

- On Days 20, 30, and 40, you might have the class help decide on a new color for the next 10 squares. (No color should be used more than once until Day 101 when the color used for Days 1 to 10 reappears.)
- To help children relate the numbers on the Counting Tape to the numbers they see, hear, and use in their daily life in and out of school, play the game *Can You Find Me, 11 to 20?* On a large piece of construction paper the same color as the numbers 11–20 on the Counting Tape note the children's observations ("John has 16 crayons in his box," "There are 14 girls and 13 boys here today," and so on) with a few words or a picture.
- Children have fun solving Counting Tape Puzzles that help them develop number sense. Provide an empty 20-space counting tape made by cutting apart and connecting four strips of five squares from Every Day Graph (TR15). Children draw 1–20 Date Cards (TR2) two at a time from a sack and place them in the correct spaces on the tape until the "puzzle" is completed. Observing how they decide where to put the numbers provides insight into their thinking.
- If you make a set of Ten Grids Cards for 1 to 10, they can be used to practice instant recognition and to help children see the numbers 6 to 9 as a group of five plus extras.
- Children can create their own flash cards for 5 + 1, 5 + 2, 5 + 3, 5 + 4, and 5 + 5 by coloring dots on copies of Ten Grids (TR9) and recording facts without the sums on the back.
- Some teachers also give children five Domino Blanks (TR6) to make Domino flash cards with five dots on one side and one to five dots on the other.

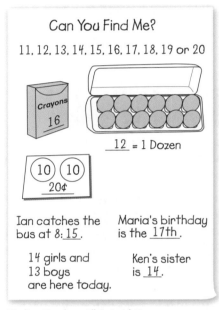

Finding Numbers All Around Us

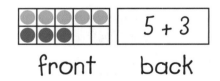

Ten Grids Flash Cards

CLOCK

Concepts & Skills

- Experience duration
- Understand analog and digital clocks
- Learn how many minutes in an hour
- Count by fives and ones
- Read the minute hand

Daily Routine

- Continue to move the minute hand forward one minute each day of school.
- On the 30th day of school point out that the hand is halfway around the Clock.

Ongoing Assessment

1. Count by fives to 35.
2. Show the Clock set to 27 after. How many minutes have gone by on this Clock? How do you know?
3. Show me 42 minutes on the Clock.

DISCUSSION

For Day 30

Day 30 is a good time to estimate how many minute marks are on the entire Clock, and to fold the blank Clock (TR12) in half to show half of a circle. Encourage children to make some estimates and then count on together from minute mark 31 to minute mark 60 to find the exact number of minutes shown on the Clock.

To help children develop a sense of how long a half hour is, you might list a few television programs and regular school activities that are a half-hour long.

"We're halfway around. How many minutes to get all the way around?"

HELPFUL HINTS

- Designate some days for catching the classroom clock when its minute hand matches the minutes on the bulletin board Clock. Use the classroom clock to help children read the hour hand first and then the minutes.

- Many children enjoy playing a game called *Clock Race*. Children will each need a copy of the Clock (TR12), 2 different color crayons and a 1–6 dot cube. Players take turns rolling the cube and coloring in that many minutes on the Clock. After each turn, player's alternate colors to help them keep track of the new minutes being added. The first player to color in 30 minutes wins. Before each roll, players must state the total number of minutes colored on their Clocks.

- On Day 30, you might find setting a kitchen timer or digital alarm clock for the next 30-minute interval a helpful reminder to read the classroom clock.

- You may wish to discuss the position of the hour hand when the minute hand is at the 30-minute mark.

- Some teachers record the days of school with tally marks by the Clock to show another way to count by fives and ones.

Tally
卌 5   卌 25
卌 10   卌 30
卌 15 ||||
卌 20

"Tally marks show another way to count by fives and ones."

GRAPH

Concepts & Skills

- Collect and record data on a graph over time
- Read and interpret data on a picture or bar graph
- Count and compare small quantities

Materials for October

Graph paper (TR15), Weather Markers (TR16)

Author Notes

"The Graph offers a different opportunity each month for the class to gather, organize, and analyze quantitative data. The weather will be recorded with picture graphs in October, January, and April, providing a sample of each season's weather to compare.

Children's preference polls, birthday data and solid collections will be some of the topics for graphing in other months. While the subject of the Graph changes from month to month, each month's accumulating data provides frequent opportunities for counting and making comparisons. The Graph provides children with math they can see and talk about."

Daily Routine

- Each day have the class look outside and decide what the weather is like at that moment. (It's best to make these observations at a similar time each day.)
- Have a volunteer attach the appropriate weather symbol to the Graph.
- Discuss the accumulating data once a week.

DISCUSSION

For the First Day

Problem Solving Instead of preparing the Weather Graph ahead of time, consider involving children in the problem-solving experience of setting it up. Show them the Weather Markers and explain that they will use some of them to keep track of the weather on a graph this month and later in the winter and spring.

Have the class help decide which of the symbols are most appropriate for use in your region. Choosing just four or five conditions to monitor through the three seasons will make the Graph easier for children to read and analyze.

After choosing the categories, help the class estimate how many squares are needed for each weather condition.

- Do we need one square for each school day in October?
- Is it possible that it might be sunny every day or rainy every day?

Ongoing Assessment

1. What does the graph this month tell about?
2. How many days have been _____? How do you know?
3. How many more days have been _____ than _____? How do you know?

October Morning Weather Sample

"How many days' weather are shown on the Graph?"

After the size of the Graph has been established, children can look for possible places in the room to display it. The space chosen may determine whether the data should be displayed vertically or horizontally. Finally, children can decide how to label the rows or columns using the chosen weather symbols and place the first marker for the day's weather on the Graph.

For During the Month

Counting, Comparing Once a week focus on the accumulating October weather data. To involve the class in counting and comparing, you might ask questions similar to these:

- What kind of weather have we had most often?
- How many sunny days have we graphed so far this month?
- Is there any kind of weather we haven't seen on school days yet?
- Does our sample show more cloudy days or sunny days? How many more?
- How many school days would it need to rain for the rainy days to equal the cloudy days?
- How many days' weather are shown on the Graph?
- Does our Graph show all days in October to this day?

HELPFUL HINTS

- Children can help color the symbols. Agree on the colors for the weather symbols beforehand so the categories will appear uniform. A variety of colors of clouds, for example, would make the number of clouds in all more difficult to see at a glance.
- While the Weather Graph has been presented here as a picture graph, it could be done as a symbolic graph, if you prefer. Children can mark the Graph by pasting or pinning up colored paper squares, writing Xs, or shading in the squares with crayons. Plan on using the same format for the winter and spring Weather Graphs so the data from the different seasons can be easily compared.

Every Day Calendar

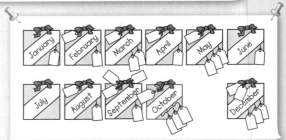

Birthday Data

2 5 rocks

Daily Depositor

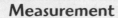

Measurement

5 6

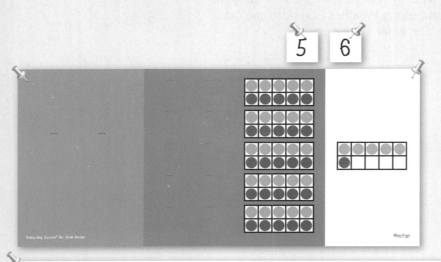

Counting Tape and Ten Grids

Clock

| 39 | 40 | 41 | 42 | 43 | 44 | 45 | 46 | 47 | 48 | 49 | 50 | 51 | 52 | 53 | 54 | 55 | 56 |

Ben had 4 pennies
and Jasmine had 3.
How many more pennies
did Ben have?
4 − 3 = 1

Number Builder

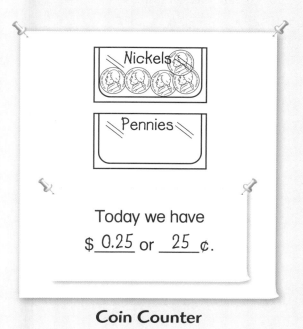

Today we have
$ 0.25 or 25 ¢.

Coin Counter

NOVEMBER ELEMENTS

In November, two new elements are added to
Calendar Math. The Coin Counter introduces
children to adding nickels and pennies. The Daily
Depositor allows children to explore another
representation of place value concepts and the
base ten counting system. The Counting Tape and
Ten Grids and Clock continue. The Calendar offers
a new pattern using two different kinds of
triangles as well as squares. Measurement uses
inches and feet to build on last month's
investigations of length. To allow more time for the
new elements, a new Graph has not been included
this month. You may want to carry on with a
November weather sample to compare with
October's.

CALENDAR

Concepts & Skills

- Recognize, analyze, and predict patterns
- Know the days of the week and months of the year in order
- Count with one-to-one correspondence to 30
- Read, compare, and order numbers to 30
- Match quantities with numerals
- Solve word problems and use mental math
- Explore and describe the attributes of triangles

Materials for the Rest of the Year

Yesterday Marker

Author Notes

"This month's pattern uses two different triangles, the equilateral and the right isosceles triangles. The variety in these two triangles will stimulate discussion about the shape and its characteristics. Explain that any shape with three straight sides and three corners is a triangle. Since the square is a special rectangle, you may consider referring to it as a "square rectangle." You and your class can determine the appropriateness of this language.

Many teachers like to have children interpret the Calendar pattern with different materials. Focus on a variety of attributes such as color, shape, texture, and size when patterning."

Daily Routine

- Note that November is the next to last (11th) month of the year.
- Place the November Birthday Package near the Calendar and invite children to find where the tags should be placed.
- Update daily. On Mondays, add pieces for Saturday and Sunday.
- Help the class read the day of the week and date using the Calendar. Place the Today Marker above the day's name and mark the previous day of the week with the Yesterday Marker.
- After a week or more, ask children to predict what color the day's piece and future pieces will be.

The November Calendar Pieces use green triangles and orange squares (square rectangles) to create an AAB pattern in the order of green triangle, green triangle, orange square (square rectangle).

DISCUSSION

For the Third and Fourth Weeks

The following questions might be helpful to elicit discussion among the children.

Geometry To explore the attributes of triangles and squares (square rectangles):

- How are the green pieces that we have put up the same?
- Are they all triangles ?
- What is a triangle? (any closed shape with 3 straight sides)
- How are the green and orange shapes the same? (They both have straight sides.)
- Do any of these pieces have "square corners" that go "straight out and straight up" or that look like the letter L? (All the squares do, but some of the triangles also have one square corner.

Number Sense To foster an understanding of ordinal numbers and the relationship of numbers through counting:

- What number and shape do we see on the 3rd Wednesday? 2nd Tuesday? 1st Monday?
- How many triangles do we have so far?
- Do we have more triangles or squares?
- Which number is greater, 7 or 17? How do you know?
- So far we have had 3 days this week. How many days are left in the week? How could we show this with a number sentence?

Algebraic Thinking To encourage searching for patterns:

- Is this a pattern? Why? (It copies itself; it repeats; it happens over and over.)
- What part of the pattern are we copying over and over?

Throughout the month, you may want to build a pattern "train" which reflects the AAB pattern appearing on the Calendar. As discussed in the previous month, some teachers like to rest this train on the chalk tray and add to it daily. Continue to encourage children to suggest ways of interpreting the month's pattern using body motions.

Analyzing Data Occasionally have children focus on the Birthday data. As children respond to your questions, listen to those willing to share how they came to their conclusions.

- How many days until the next birthday?
- How much older is one November birthday child than another?
- Are there more birthdays this month or in your birthday month?
- How many months until your birthday month arrives?
- I see 2 months next to each other where the tags have a sum of 7. Which 2 months could these be?

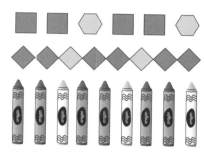

AAB Pattern Trains

November Patterns

The pattern goes green, green, orange.

The orange go down like stairs.

It goes two triangles, one square, two triangles one square.

The oranges go 3, 6, 9, 12, 15, 18, 21, 24, 27, 30.

It is an AAB, AAB pattern.

The green, green, orange copies itself.

To Sum Up

To wrap up the month's discussion of the Calendar pattern, ask children to tell some of the things they have noticed about the Calendar this month.

You might also want to play *Find the Missing Piece* by removing three or four pieces from the Calendar and inviting the children to guess which one of them you are thinking of. "Math talk," as in the examples below, can be used to determine this piece.

- Is it a neighbor of 13?
- Is it a green triangle?
- Does it have three straight sides?
- Does it come between 13 and 15?
- Is it one less than 15?

HELPFUL HINT

- Sometimes, when you are chanting the color pattern on the Calendar or doing body motions to the pattern, switch over to saying AAB, AAB. If the children are used to describing the patterns with a variety of words (triangle, triangle, square, or lettuce, lettuce, carrot, or clap, clap, snap), letters will simply be one more way to describe them.

Number & Operations   Algebra   Geometry   Measurement   Data & Probability
Problem Solving   Reasoning   Communication   Connections   Representation

NUMBER BUILDER

Concepts & Skills

- Understand processes of addition and subtraction
- Use the language of addition and subtraction (take away and comparison)
- Discuss part and whole relationships for 7
- Use symbolic notation to record addition and subtraction
- Match quantities and numerals
- Share number stories

Daily Routine

- During the first two weeks of this month, allow a volunteer to count out 7 counters and choose how to distribute them between the two pockets.
- Encourage children to break up the group in new ways, so that all possibilities are explored.
- Occasionally look at a comparison subtraction suggested by the counters in the pockets.
- Two or three times a week record a story in words and with symbols.
- Toward the end of the month, play *Make a Match* for sums of 7. (See October, page 38.)

Ongoing Assessment

1. What are two ways we can make 7?
2. Which pocket has more counters? How many more?
3. If we put 4 counters in the top pocket, how many will we need to put in the bottom pocket?

DISCUSSION

For Throughout the Month

Refer to October's Discussion for specific suggestions (page 37). During the last week of November, when Number Builder is set up for *Make a Match* with Domino Cards 1 through 6, a discussion similar to the following might occur.

Sample Dialogue

Teacher: What sum are we working with this month?

Class: 7.

Teacher: Who will be our first volunteer to search for a sum for 7?

Child: (turning over two cards) I got a 5 and a 1. That makes 6, but we want to make 7.

Teacher: Let's try it again. If you could turn over any two numbers, which ones would you want?

Child: I would like 6 and 1. That's an easy one!

Teacher: Okay, let's see what you get.

Child: I got a 5 and a 2. Let's see 1, 2, 3, 4, 5, 6, 7. This makes 7.

Teacher: Is there another way that we could figure that out?

Child: I started at 5 and counted 6, 7.

Teacher: He counted on. Let's try that, beginning with 5.

Class: Five, 6, 7.

Teacher: We know that 5 and 2 make 7 or 5 and 2 is the same as 7. Who would be willing to search for another match?

You might want to save any recording of matches for the end of the game. After all matches have been made, ask the children to help you make a list of all the ways that you made 7.

HELPFUL HINTS

- If the permanent Domino Cards for review have not yet been made, you may want to do so at this time (gluing the 2 Domino Halves equalling 7 on a Domino background).

- You will now have sets for fives, sixes, and sevens. Play *Quick as You Can* with these cards. Sort them by +0, +1, +2 to search for patterns when adding 0, 1, and 2. Hold up the Domino Card for the children to state the sum "quick as they can" and then turn it around. Is the sum for 2 + 5 the same as 5 + 2? Children have fun with these "turn arounds."

- Select materials to use as counters that might also provide great sorting opportunities. For example, if rocks or shells are used, you might introduce the collection by asking, "Can someone tell us one thing you notice about the rocks?" When a child offers, "Some are shiny," you might follow with, "Yes. Are they all shiny?" Then sort them into the "shiny" and "not shiny" piles. To keep suggestions coming, push the rocks back together after each sorting and ask, "Can anyone tell us something else you notice about the rocks?" Children will discover many ways the objects are alike and different and increase their descriptive vocabulary by listening to each other.

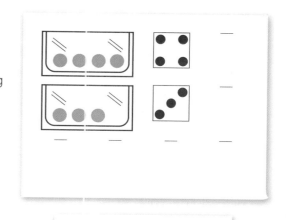

Ben had 4 pennies
and Jasmine had 3.
How many more pennies
did Ben have?
4 − 3 = 1

"5 and 1 make 6 and we are searching for 7. I need to turn these cards back over."

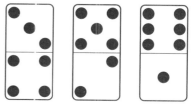

Permanent Domino Cards for 7

DAILY DEPOSITOR

Concepts & Skills

- Count with one-to-one correspondence
- Match quantities and numerals
- Compare quantities to 31
- Read numerals to 31
- Group and count by tens
- Understand place value
- Understand processes of addition and subtraction
- Use symbolic notation to record addition and subtraction

Materials for the Year

Depositor poster, four 3" × 6" clear pockets, a supply of paper recording sheets; 0–9 Digit Cards (TR10); 30 small rocks or other counters

Author Notes

"Each month the Daily Depositor displays a number of counters, grouped by tens and ones, equal to the day's date. Starting on the first of the month, a volunteer adds a counter each day to the ones side of the Depositor. On the tenth of the month when 10 counters are collected on the ones side, they are gathered into one group of ten which is moved to a pocket on the tens side. So, on the 10th, 20th, and 30th days of the month, children observe the digit in the tens place change to match the number of tens in the Depositor.

The main purpose of this place-value activity is to help children see and talk about quantities to 30, developing versatility with these amounts. Unlike Ten Grids that explores larger numbers in a place-value format, the Depositor continually revisits the smaller numbers through 31, providing children with many opportunities to match these quantities with numerals. Each month for the next four months, the place-value model will change. Repeated exposure to the "teen" numbers and the value of their places contributes to a better understanding of these numbers. This month, rocks or small counters are collected and grouped by tens and ones."

Daily Routine

- Add one counter each day to the ones pocket. On Mondays, always add counters for Saturday and Sunday so the total in the Depositor is the same as the day's date.
- Whenever 10 counters accumulate, put them into a new pocket on the tens side.
- Record the total, read the number, and have the class help you identify how many groups of ten and how many leftover ones there are.

Daily Depositor on Day 25

DISCUSSION

For Throughout the Month

The following discussion might occur in your classroom on the 15th of the month.

Sample Dialogue

Teacher: How many counters do we have in the Depositor today?

Class: We have 15.

Teacher: How can we be sure that there are 15?

Child: We can count them 1, 2, 3, 4, . . . , 15.

Teacher: That always works. Besides counting each one, is there another way that we could count them?

Child: I know that there are 10 in this pocket, so I counted ten, 11, 12, 13, 14, 15.

Teacher: Let's all try counting on from 10.

Teacher & Class: Ten, 11, 12, 13, 14, 15.

Teacher: Do our numerals match our counters?

Child: No, our numbers show 14, we need to change the 4 to a 5.

Teacher: Now that our numbers show 15, what does this (pointing to the 1) tell us?

Class: We have 1 group of ten.

Teacher: (pointing to the 5) And what does this tell us?

Class: We have 5 extra ones.

Teacher: So 10 in this pocket and 5 more here in this pocket make 15. Is that right?

Continue to explore the different ways of counting the quantity in the Depositor and connecting the numerals to the counters. Break the quantity apart to look at the tens plus the ones. Take time to emphasize that 16 ones is the same as one group of ten and 6 extra ones. This aspect of conservation, that one group of ten is the same as ten extra ones, needs to be revisited frequently.

HELPFUL HINT

- *Fill Up Ten and Then Again to 30* is a good independent extension for counting tens and ones. Each player uses three of the blank Ten Grids. Players take turns tossing the cube and placing that number of counters on a grid. The grids should be filled left to right across the top and then across the bottom. Players must tell how many counters they have in all before each toss. The first player to fill three grids wins.

MEASUREMENT

Concepts & Skills
- Measure length in nonstandard and standard units (inches)
- Match 12 inches with a foot ruler

Materials for November
Three 3" × 10" strips of Inch Squared Paper (TR17); watercolor pens in two colors; tape, tack, and common objects of varying lengths

Author Notes
"In this element, children will have the opportunity to join in constructing a measuring tape that increases in length one inch every day of the month. This month the children will be using what they have experienced with estimating length as they learn how to use a standard measure."

Setup
Attach three 3" × 10" strips of Inch Squared Paper to form a 30-inch strip. Post it in a visible spot such as above the chalk tray or below a windowsill or counter edge.

Daily Routine
- Each day color in one square inch along the center row of the tape. On Mondays, color inches for both Saturday and Sunday also.
- Alternate colors every five squares to make it easier to read from a distance.
- Record the day's measurement near the tape. "Today the length of our tape measure is _____ inches."
- Discuss briefly each day until the 12th of the month and twice a week in later weeks.

DISCUSSION

For Early in the Month
As often as possible, include an estimation activity. Have children look around the room for objects that might match the colored inches on the tape for the day. Allow two or three children to bring up objects they have found. Before each object is matched to the tape, ask the class to predict if it will be too long, too short, or just right (within a half inch). If an object's length matches the day's tape to the nearest inch, it remains next to the tape for all to see throughout the day. If none of the objects are close enough, do not place anything by the tape at this time. Perhaps something will be found during the day.

Ongoing Assessment
1. Is your pencil longer than, shorter than, or equal to the length of the ruler?
2. Can you use our measuring tape to tell me how long this pencil is?
3. Show me an object that is longer than 10 inches.

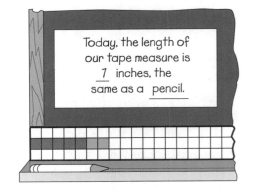

Today, the length of our tape measure is _7_ inches, the same as a pencil.

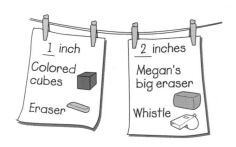

1 inch
Colored cubes

Eraser

2 inches
Megan's big eraser

Whistle

For the Twelfth of the Month

If no one suggests a ruler to match the tape's length on this day, bring one out and place it on the tape so children can see that the ruler is exactly 12 inches long. Devote all of Calendar Math time on this day to measuring. Pass out rulers, and let children measure the length of their own feet to compare to the standard foot ruler. They may need to be reminded to line up their heel with the "zero" end of the ruler.

The following questions promote comparing and measuring.

- Is your shoe longer than, shorter than, or equal to the ruler?
- Is your shoe more than 12 inches, less than 12 inches, or equal to 12 inches?
- Can you find something in the room longer than a foot or 12 inches? Something shorter than a foot or 12 inches?

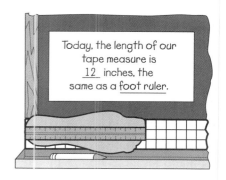

Today, the length of our tape measure is 12 inches, the same as a foot ruler.

For Later in the Month

As the length of the tape increases, finding objects to match becomes difficult. Instead, have the class guess and check the length of a common object drawn from a collection box of items (paintbrush, ribbon, scissors, etc.). After estimates have been made, a volunteer matches one end of the object exactly with the end of the tape and reads the tape to the nearest inch.

HELPFUL HINTS

- On the 12th, some teachers glue a ruler to a 12-inch cardboard foot cutout that can rest on the measuring tape throughout the day. This helps everyone remember that the 12-inch ruler is equal to one "foot."
- Sometimes children suggest objects that cannot be brought to the tape (a drawer handle, paper towel holder, etc.). They can cut string equal to the length of the object they cannot pick up and bring the string to the tape to measure. String also works well for checking the length of curves.

Number & Operations		Algebra	Geometry	Measurement	Data & Probability	
Problem Solving		Reasoning	Communication	Connections	Representation	

COUNTING TAPE AND TEN GRIDS

Concepts & Skills

- Group and count by tens, fives, and ones
- Understand place value
- Compare and order quantities
- Count on and count back
- See number patterns
- Use the language of duration
- Think of 6 to 9 as a group of five plus extra ones
- Add or subtract 10
- See 50 as half of 100

Ongoing Assessment

1. How many more dots or squares do we need to get to 50?
2. How many groups of ten squares do we see today? How many extra ones?
3. If we add 10 to today's amount what will we have? What will we have if we take off a full ten grid?

Materials for November

A Hundred Chart (TR20) or a meterstick

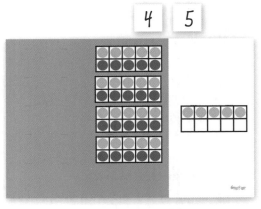

"If we take away a full Ten Grid we'll have 35. If we add a ten we'll have 55."

Daily Routine

- Continue to add one square to the Counting Tape and one dot to the Ten Grids for each day of school.
- Adapt questions from September and October to the larger numbers and quantities now appearing to encourage comparing, counting on, counting back, and counting by tens and ones, or tens, fives, and ones.

DISCUSSION

For During the Month

Place Value, Ordering By the 40th day of school, children will have observed the counting sequence from 1 to 10 repeated 4 times. Here are some questions that help children see that they can use what they know about sets of 10 to work with higher numbers.

- Can you all find Day 4 on the Tape? Day 14? Day 24?
- What number did we put up 3 days after Day 4? Three days after Day 14? Three days after Day 24?
- Do you notice anything alike about all our answers? (They all have a 7.)
- Why are we always getting a 7? (4 and 3 more makes 7.)
- What day came one day before Day 8? One day before Day 18? One day before Day 28? One day before Day 38?
- Do you notice anything alike about all our answers? (They all have a 7 in them.)
- Why do we keep getting 7? (It always comes just before 8.)
- So what day will come up one day before we get to Day 58? Day 68?

For the Fiftieth Day of School

Number Sense Day 50 provides an appropriate occasion to explore the idea of 50 being halfway to 100. Since only the first 50 numbers are in view on the Tape, the class will need to look at another visual aid that shows the entire span from 1 to 100. The Hundred Chart or a meterstick will do. Coloring half the Chart will show 1 to 50 in the top half and 51 to 100 in the bottom half, helping children see 50 as half of 100. Counting centimeters by tens to the end of the meterstick and then counting again to the midpoint will also show 50 to be halfway to 100. Then ask children to guess how far the Counting Tape will stretch by Day 100. Compare to the estimates they made last month.

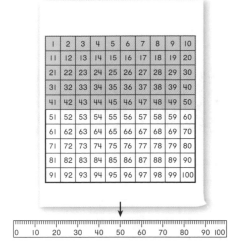

Halfway to 100

HELPFUL HINTS

- On Day 50, introduce the game *1–50 Chart Race*. Players take turns tossing two 0–5 cubes, stating the sum, and crossing out that number of squares on their own Hundred Chart (TR20). Players must tell before they toss the total number of squares crossed out and then take their turn. The first to cross out 50 wins.

-  Larger numbers present an excellent opportunity to let children explore with their calculators. During Counting Tape and Ten Grids discussions, occasionally let children verify their answers on a calculator.

Number & Operations	Algebra	Geometry	Measurement	Data & Probability
Problem Solving	Reasoning	Communication	Connections	Representation

COIN COUNTER

Concepts & Skills

- Know the penny and nickel
- Count by fives and ones
- Determine the value of a collection of coins
- Use mental math, including figuring change
- Record money amounts using both the dollar sign with decimal point and the cent sign

Ongoing Assessment

1. How many pennies can you get for a nickel?

2. A nickel and two pennies equals how many cents?

3. Three nickels equals how many cents?

Materials for the Year

Two 3" × 6" clear pockets, one labeled nickels and one labeled pennies; penny and nickel demonstration coins; 6 nickel and 10 penny Coin Cards (TR22), or the same number of real nickels and pennies

Author Notes

"The Coin Counter activities help children incrementally develop the skill of counting money by tens, fives, and ones. Adding a penny to the Coin Counter each day of November, children represent the date in nickels and pennies, trading pennies for a nickel whenever possible."

Daily Routine

- Each day place one penny into the penny pocket so the value in the Coin Counter always matches the date. On Mondays add pennies for Saturday and Sunday also.

- When five pennies accumulate, trade them for a nickel to put into the nickel pocket.

- When the next penny is added, model counting the nickel as five and counting on one more to six. Thereafter count the total each day by fives and ones, clapping on the last five. For example, on the 18th, say, "5, 10, 15 (clap), 16, 17, 18 cents."

- Record the total cents below the Coin Counter in both the dollar sign with decimal point form and the cent sign form so the children can become familiar with each.

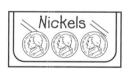

Today we have
$ 0.18 or 18 ¢.

DISCUSSION

For the First Day

Display the large demonstration coins that show both sides of the nickel and the penny and give a real nickel and penny to each child. Ask children to look at the coins in their hands and the pictures to find some things that are alike on the nickel and penny. (Their observations will give you some openings to interject information about the two Presidents, the buildings, and the coins.)

"How are the coins alike? How are they different?"

Sample Dialogue

Teacher: What do you notice about the coins?

Child: They both have faces.

Child: The penny is Lincoln.

Child: The nickel is different.

Teacher: The face on the nickel is Thomas Jefferson, the third President. He lived at the same time as George Washington, over 200 years ago. What else do you see?

Child: They both have buildings.

Teacher: That is true. The building on the back of the nickel is Jefferson's home at Monticello, Virginia. It's where he lived except for when he was President. Now, look at the building on the penny. It is the Lincoln Memorial, built after President Lincoln died to honor him and his ideas. So the nickel and penny both show people and buildings. Are they alike in any other ways?

Child: They both have numbers.

Child: The numbers tell when they were made.

Teacher: Now can we find some ways the two are different?

Child: The nickel is bigger.

Child: They are different colors.

Teacher: Yes, the orange-brown penny is covered with copper metal, which gives it this color. The nickel is covered with nickel, a metal that gives it the silver-gray color.

Getting to know the nickel and penny in this way, while time consuming, should help children keep the coins straight later when they are working with dimes and quarters as well. To wrap up such a discussion, collect the nickels and pennies from the children for future use in the Coin Counter.

For Throughout the Month

Mental Math Asking some of the following questions now and then during the month will make the Coin Counter a focus for mathematical thinking.

- How many coins are in our Counter?
- How many more days until we get the next nickel?
- How many days until we have 20¢?
- How many pennies can you get for 2 nickels?
- If we bought a pencil for 12¢, how much would we have left?

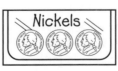

Today we have
$ 0.18 or 18 ¢.

HELPFUL HINT

- The use of real coins is encouraged whenever possible. Telling the class you trust them to take care of your coins so that they can be used over and over during the year may help the class to meet your expectations.

CLOCK

Concepts & Skills

- Experience duration
- Understand analog and digital clocks
- Learn how many minutes are in an hour
- Count by fives and ones
- Read the minute and hour hands

Ongoing Assessment

1. Count for me by fives to 45.
2. How many minutes are in half an hour?
3. Show me where 57 minutes is on the Clock.

Daily Routine

- Continue to move the minute hand of the Clock forward 1 minute each day of school.
- Read aloud and record the time.

DISCUSSION

For During the Month

Catching the minute hand on the classroom clock when it matches the one on the bulletin board Clock and then reading the hour and minutes together will help avoid the potential confusion when interpreting the hour hand. Ask the class to tell you how to show the hour hand on the bulletin board Clock at these times. Gradually more children will notice that no matter how close the hour hand is to the next hour, it isn't that hour until the minute hand is straight up. Each day the class can figure out how many minutes until the hour by looking at the updated Clock.

HELPFUL HINTS

- A geared demonstration clock can be used to show how the hour hand moves ever so slowly ahead just one hour each time the minute hand goes all the way around.
- If your class reaches the 60th day of school in November, look ahead to the Clock Discussion for Day 60 on pages 70–71.

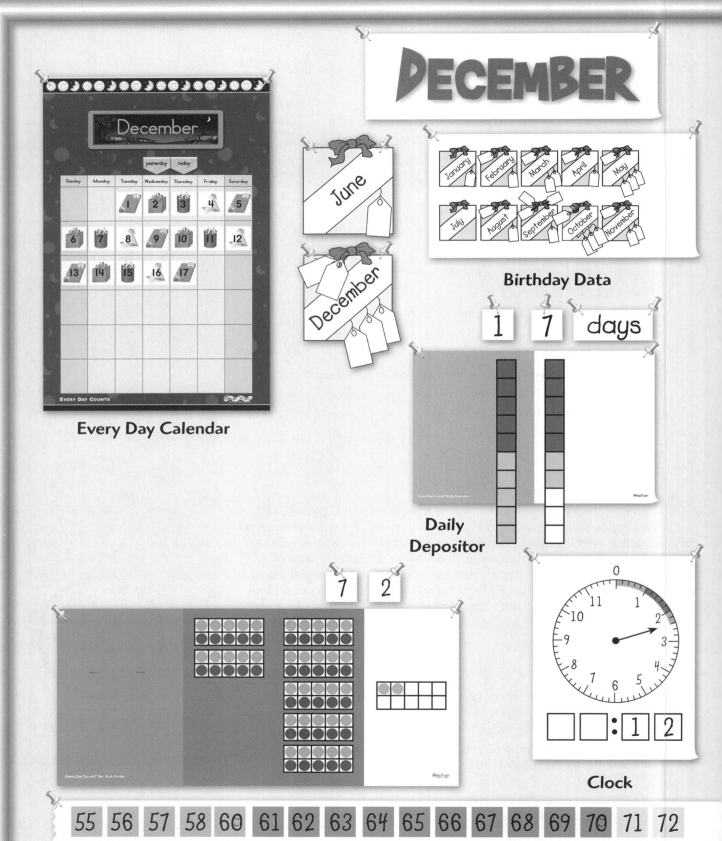

Every Day Calendar

DECEMBER

Birthday Data

Daily Depositor

Clock

Counting Tape and Ten Grids

8 cats were on the fence
but 3 cats jumped down.
How many cats were left
on the fence?

$8 - 3 = 5$

Number Builder

Today we have

$ _0.17_ or _17_ ¢.

Coin Counter

DECEMBER ELEMENTS

December is often hectic. To minimize teacher preparation, there are no new elements introduced this month. There is also no Measurement or Graph element suggested this month.

You'll notice that the December holidays do not play a part in Calendar Math since views differ widely as to the role holidays should play in schools. If your school is one in which these holidays are incorporated into the classroom, you might want to adapt the Calendar and Number Builder stories to reflect them.

CALENDAR

Concepts & Skills

- Recognize, analyze, and predict patterns
- Know the days of the week and months of the year in order
- Count with one-to-one correspondence to 31
- Read, compare, and order numbers to 31
- Count on and count back
- Match quantities with numerals
- Explore and describe the attributes of rectangular solids, cylinders, and cones
- Interpret organized data
- Solve problems

Ongoing Assessment

1. What pattern do you see on the Calendar?
2. Describe the box shapes.
3. Which shapes do you think would roll? Why?

Author Notes

"This month's pattern will also allow many interpretations, depending on the background of your children. The rectangular box and cube-shaped box that are both rectangular solids may stimulate discussion or may simply be referred to as box shapes. The colors of the shapes, the three-dimensional shapes themselves, and the color of the ribbons provide several patterns. You may want to search for items in the environment that represent these three-dimensional shapes and collect them for use in your classroom. Explore the shapes that roll, slide, and stack."

Daily Routine

- **The first day,** take December's Birthday Package out of the array and feature it near the Calendar. If you have decided to recognize summer vacation birthdays on those children's half-year birthdays, you will need to bring down the June Package as well. (See September Helpful Hints, page 31.)

- Have the class predict where both the birthdays and half-year "unbirthdays" will appear on the Calendar and mark them all with the tags taken from the Birthday Packages.

- Each day after a pattern appears have children predict the shape, color, or ribbon color for the day's Calendar Piece.

The December Calendar Pieces show a green box, blue cube-shaped box, red can or cylinder, and yellow party hat or cone to create an ABCD pattern. Ribbons on each of these shapes also create a pattern and indicate the color of the next package.

DISCUSSION

For the Beginning of the Month

At the beginning of December, ask the class to point out the Birthday Package that matches the month written above the Calendar. Have the class name all the months in order, beginning this chant with the January Package. Then go through the sequence again, stopping with a clap on the present month. Note that December is the 12th and last month of the year. After reminding everyone of this year's number, let children predict the number for the new year that will appear when everyone returns from their December break.

Adapt questions from previous months to bring attention to the winding down of one calendar year and the upcoming new year beginning January 1.

Mental Math, Problem Solving To find differences:

- How many days until the next birthday?
- How many days until the year ends?
- How many days until the end of the month?
- How many days until New Year's Day?

DISCUSSION

For the Second Week

Continue to discuss and make predictions with December's patterns. Bring out some three-dimensional shapes from your classroom collection for the class to explore. Look for shapes similar to the Calendar shapes. A discussion similar to the following might occur.

Sample Dialogue

Teacher: What do you notice about the green and blue shapes?

Class: They both look like boxes. They have corners. They have ribbons.

Teacher: What do you notice about the sides of these boxes?

Class: Some are long. Some are big. Some are little. Some are the same size.

Teacher: In the world of mathematics, we call the flat sides of boxes faces .

Teacher: Do you think that the boxes in our shape collection would stack or roll?

Child: They would stack since they are flat.

Child: They have flat faces!

Teacher: You're right. Do we have any shapes in our collection that you think might roll? Let's check and see.

Child: These cans roll since they are round. This ice cream cone also rolls. It's kind of round, too.

Teacher: Do any of our classroom shapes look like our Calendar shapes? Could you tell which of our Calendar shapes might stack and which ones might roll?

Child: The Calendar shapes go stack, stack, roll, roll, stack, stack, roll, roll. That could be a pattern.

Continue to look for different ways to describe these shapes and to see what other patterns might evolve. Corners and no corners, flat and curved, and circles and no circles might all be suggestions for sorting and patterning. Continue to ask the following types of questions.

Algebraic Thinking To search for patterns:

- What patterns do you see? How would you describe them?
- How can you convince us that these are patterns?
- What is happening with our ribbons?

"The pattern was green, blue, red, yellow, green, blue, red, yellow."

"The pattern was present, present, present, party hat over and over."

"It keeps going stack, stack, roll, roll."

For Just Prior to December Vacation

Problem Solving The mid-month break for vacation offers a special opportunity for children to use their evolving understanding of patterns to help predict the rest of the month's Calendar Pieces. Pointing out the space for the last day of the month and asking, "What color will appear here?" will evoke a variety of problem-solving approaches on the children's part. Allow time for several children to show on the Calendar how they came up with their prediction. Let children predict and put up the Calendar Pieces for other December days until the entire month's pieces are up.

HELPFUL HINTS

- Some teachers like to have a box of the three-dimensional shapes used in the Calendar for the children to continue exploring. These shapes from the environment allow additional experiences for children to look at the similarities and differences among the shapes. Children can investigate the faces and corners of these shapes. They can determine which shapes roll, slide, and stack and why this occurs.

- Agree on a day just prior to vacation to recognize any children whose birthdays will occur during vacation. Any children who have a January birthday before school resumes can be recognized on the first day back from vacation, when the January Package is brought down from the array and its tags are placed on the January Calendar.

- Children might enjoy making a paper chain with a link to represent each day remaining in December. Some children might want to see the month's color pattern incorporated into the chain. A link can be removed and those that are left recounted each morning. Another way to count down is to write the numbers from 1 to the total days left on an inch-squared-paper strip (TR17) and cut off or cross out one number a day until only the square labeled *1* remains on December 31. If time allows for children to make their own chain or countdown strip sometime prior to vacation, they can take it home and share the routine with their families.

| 1 | 2 | 3 | 4 | 5 | 6 | 7 | 8 | 9 | 10 | 11 | 12 | 13 | 14 | 15 | 16 |

End of Year Countdown Strip

Number & Operations	Algebra	Geometry	Measurement	Data & Probability
Problem Solving	Reasoning	Communication	Connections	Representation

NUMBER BUILDER

Concepts & Skills
- Understand the processes of addition and subtraction
- Use the language of addition and subtraction (take away and comparison)
- Discuss part and whole relationships for 8
- See patterns in addition and subtraction
- Use symbolic notation to record addition and subtraction
- Match quantities and numerals
- Share number stories

Ongoing Assessment
1. Which is greater, 3 or 5? How do you know?
2. Six is how much more than 2?
3. Can you tell me a comparing story about the counters you see?

Daily Routine

- For the first two weeks of the month, allow a volunteer to count out 8 counters and choose how to place them into the two pockets. Be sure all the combinations get explored.
- Clip corresponding Domino Halves to the right of the pockets to duplicate each sum.
- Have children share stories to correspond to the numbers of counters. Record a few stories with number sentences for the class to read later.
- The last two weeks, play *Make the Sum* or *Make a Match* for sums of 8. (See Discussion.)

DISCUSSION

For During the Month

Mental Math, Addition and Subtraction Concepts Here are some questions you might ask to focus on adding, taking away, and comparing problems as well as the combinations for 8:

- Who has an adding story to share with us? A take away story?
- We just wrote 5 + 3 = 8 for our story. Where did the 5 come from? What does the 8 tell us?
- What do we do when we compare?
- I have a comparing story to share. I have 5 puppies and my neighbor has 3. How many more puppies do I have?
- Does anyone have a comparing story to tell us?
- What do we need to add to 5 to get to 8?
- How can we break 8 apart?

For the last week in December, before winter break, select any of the activities from previous months. At the end of the month, create permanent Domino Cards to show all the combinations for 8.

8 cats were on the fence but 3 cats jumped down. How many cats were left on the fence?
8 – 3 = 5

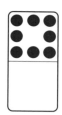 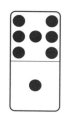 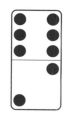 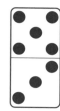 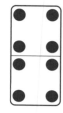

Add the five Domino Cards for 8 to your collection.

HELPFUL HINTS

- *Double-Draw Comparing* with Dominoes 1 through 4 is an option as an independent extension of Number Builder. Each player draws two Domino Halves cards at a time. The players add the dots on both cards and state their sum. *(Four plus two is six* or *three plus one is four.)* The player with the larger sum takes all four cards after stating the comparison of the sums. *(Six is greater than four.)*
- Children can create their own number storybook by drawing counter pictures and telling their own stories about the counters to a partner or parents later at home. You may want to use the Box Backgrounds (TR26). Children might create stories for sums of 5, 6, 7, or 8 and sort them by the sum or by the addends. Story records can be collected into booklets and kept in the classroom library for future browsing.

DAILY DEPOSITOR

Concepts & Skills

- Count with one-to-one correspondence
- Match quantities and numerals
- Compare quantities and read numerals to 31
- Group and count by tens
- Understand place value
- Understand processes of addition and subtraction
- Use symbolic notation to record addition and subtraction

Materials for December

Four 1" × 10" paper strips (from TR17); a blue and a red crayon

Author Notes

"This month's Daily Depositor uses blank paper strips of ten units which are colored in, one unit per day. The ten-unit strip is attached to the ones side of the Depositor and on the tenth day when it has been completely colored in, it will be moved to the tens side. The children are continually verifying that the numerals above the strips match the quantity of colored units. Prior to leaving for December break, the class will determine the number of days left in the month (and year) and color them in."

Daily Routine

- The first day, attach a blank ten strip to the ones side of the Depositor. Have a volunteer color the top unit blue.
- Each day color in one more unit. On Mondays, also color in units for Saturday and Sunday, so the total is always the same as the day's date. Alternate between red and blue every five days to make it easier to see the number of units at a glance.
- Record the number of colored units above the Depositor.
- On December 10, move the completed strip to the tens side.
- On December 11, put up a blank strip on the ones side and continue the pattern of updating.
- From the tenth on, have the class tell how many tens they see and how many extra ones they see as you record the total.

DISCUSSION

For Throughout the Month
Sample Dialogue

Once a week your class might engage in a discussion like the following one.

Teacher: How many units have been colored in so far?

Class: 17 have been colored in.

Teacher: Yes, 17. How did you know we had 17?

Child: There's 1, 2, 3, . . . , 17. And today is December 17.

Child: We can also get to seventeen by beginning at ten. Ten, 11, 12, 13, 14, 15, 16, 17.

Teacher: Let's show this with our numbers: 1 for the 1 group of ten above the tens and a 7 for the extra ones above the ones. Let's read it together.

Teacher & Class: One group of 10 and 7 make 17. Could we write 10 + 7 = 17?

Class: Yes.

Teacher: What if we took the 7 extra ones away, how many would be left?

Class: 10.

Teacher: So we started with 17 and took all of the extra ones away leaving 10. 17 − 7 = 10.

For the Last School Day before Break

Number Sense On the last day before break, put up the remaining ten strips and one extra unit to show a total of 31 units. Explain that these 31 units represent all the days in December. Some of the following questions may help to promote critical thinking and to develop counting strategies based on the display.

- How many blank units are left to be colored in this month?

- How did you get your answer?

- Did you count all the blank units or did you use a shortcut?

- If you used a shortcut, could you share it with us?

- The blank units are the days that are left in December, the last month of the year. December 31 will be the last day of the year. So how many days are left in this year?

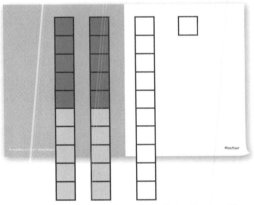
"How many days are left in the year?"

HELPFUL HINT

- By taping 2 colored ten strips together, a tape is created for the game *Tape Race*. Each player tosses the dot cube and places that number of counters on his or her tape, with one counter per square, filling the tape from left to right. Players must tell how many counters are on the tape before taking a turn. The first player to fill the tape wins.

 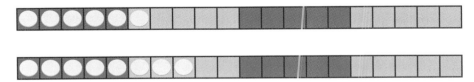

"Now it's my turn. I have 8 so far."

COUNTING TAPE AND TEN GRIDS

Concepts & Skills

- Count with one-to-one correspondence
- Group and count by tens, fives, and ones
- Understand place value
- Compare and order quantities
- Think of sets 6 to 9 as a group of five and extras
- Know addition combinations for sums 5 and 10
- Add or subtract 10
- Use number patterns to do mental math
- Use the language of duration
- Solve problems

Ongoing Assessment

1. How many more days until day _____?
2. What number is two more than 5? 15? 35?
3. Explain how you could add 7 and 7 by pulling the fives out of each seven.

Daily Routine

- Continue to add a dot to the Ten Grids and a square to the Counting Tape each day.
- Use the larger numbers and quantities to ask questions that provide children with different levels of challenge.
- When identifying the day's total number of dots, have children come up with a variety of ways to count and verify the quantity.

DISCUSSION

`60 61 62 63 64 65 66 67 68 69 70 71 72`

For During the Month

On days when 6 to 9 dots appear on the Ten Grid in the ones area ask children to state the 5+ fact illustrated. Use Ten Grid models of these numbers to explore doubling these numbers by pulling out fives to make ten and adding the extra ones.

Adapt questions from previous months to the new numbers and quantities on the Counting Tape and Ten Grids. You might relate questions to classroom events as well. For example, on Day 63, some questions might include the following.

- How many more days are there until Day 70? How did some of you decide that?
- How can the Ten Grids help us know how many more days until Day 70?
- If today's square shows number 63, what number is on the square that we put up 10 days ago? Could someone share how you got your answer?
- Julia joined our class on Day 40. About how many days has she been part of our class?
- How many squares have we added to the Tape since we put up Day 55? Since Day 45?
- What number is two more (or two less) than 13? 23? 43? 63?

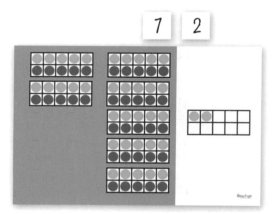

"How many days ago was Day 70?"

HELPFUL HINTS

- Children enjoy using the Counting Tape to play the game *I'm Thinking of a Number*. The teacher gives clues for a number appearing on the Counting Tape, and the children use the Tape to try to figure out the number. The clues can provide different degrees of challenge. For example:

  I'm thinking of a number that . . .

  > is 3 more than 15.

  > is the same as 3 groups of 10 and 4 more.

  > is the same as 5 and 5 and 3.

  > is 4 more minutes than half an hour.

- Play *Fill Up Tens to 50*. Play the game as introduced in the November Daily Depositor Helpful Hint, page 53, but have children play to 50 instead of 30.

Number & Operations	Algebra	Geometry	Measurement	Data & Probability
Problem Solving	Reasoning	Communication	Connections	Representation

COIN COUNTER

Concepts & Skills

- Know the penny and nickel
- Know the value of each coin and coin equivalencies
- Count by fives and ones
- Determine the value of a collection of coins
- Use mental math to figure change
- Record money amounts using both the dollar sign with decimal point and the cent sign
- Problem solve with coins

Ongoing Assessment

1. One nickel and three pennies are equal to how many cents?

2. Two nickels and two pennies equal how many cents?

3. How can you make 8 cents with nickels and pennies? How can you make 6 cents? 9 cents?

Daily Routine

- Continue to add a penny each day of school, trading for a nickel when possible.

DISCUSSION

For During the Month

Mental Math, Addition, Subtraction Questions similar to any of the following will focus attention on the coins and encourage some mental math.

- How many days until we get the next nickel?
- How much will we have on that day?
- How many nickels and pennies will there be on the 19th?
- If we take today's money to the store, can we buy a pencil for 8¢? What will our change be?
- How much more do we need to buy a sharpener for 25¢?

Today we have
$ _0.17_ or _17_ ¢.

Helpful Hints

- Thinking of 6, 7, 8, and 9 as a nickel plus one penny, a nickel plus two pennies, a nickel plus three pennies, and a nickel plus four pennies provides a powerful visual model for learning the 5+ facts. Children can then use these facts illustrated on the Coin Comparing Cards (TR24) to discover a quick way to find sums to 18 by pulling out fives.

- You might introduce *Coin Collector,* a game that children can play at home over vacation. Partners take turns tossing a 1 to 6 number cube and collecting that amount in pennies. Five pennies are traded for a nickel whenever possible. Players state their total amounts before each toss. The first player to trade for six nickels, reaching 30 cents, wins.

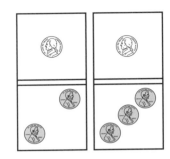

"7 is 5 + 2 and 8 is 5 +3. So 7 + 8 = 15. Take 5s from the 7 and 8 to make 10, and 2 and 3 more are 5. That's 15."

Number & Operations	Algebra	Geometry	Measurement	Data & Probability
Problem Solving	Reasoning	Communication	Connections	Representation

CLOCK

Concepts & Skills

- Experience duration
- Understand analog and digital clocks
- Learn how many minutes are in an hour
- Count by fives and ones
- Read the minute and hour hands

Materials for December

A digital clock or a kitchen timer (optional)

Daily Routine

- Continue to move the minute hand forward one minute each day as in previous months.
- On Day 60, record *00* to show zero minutes past the new hour.
- From Day 61 until December vacation, begin adding minutes for a new hour, or put the Clock aside.

DISCUSSION

For Day Sixty

Duration On Day 60, when the minute hand has finally made it all the way around the Clock, consider celebrating the concepts of one minute and one hour. This might happen by honoring each journey the minute hand makes around the classroom clock on this day by initiating one minute of silence beginning at one minute before each new hour. Children will be developing a feeling for just how long a minute is, and an hour as well.

60th day of school

If they read the clock at 9:59, 10:59, and so on throughout the day, they will gain practice reading the hour hand when it is in its most misleading position. If time allows, some other possibilities for exploring the idea of a minute and an hour might include:

- Can you jog slowly in place for one whole minute?

- How many times can we say our ABCs in one minute?

- Can you tie your shoes in one minute?

- What lasts one hour?

- If you could choose something to do with your parents or family for one whole hour, what would it be?

- If you could choose what to do at school for an hour, what would it be?

Helpful Hints

- You might want to employ a kitchen timer or digital alarm clock on the 60th day to remind everyone to look at the classroom clock just prior to the arrival of each new hour.

- Use the classroom clock to reinforce the concept of the hour hand moving ahead just one hour each time the minute hand makes its 60-minute journey around the clock.

- Children enjoy playing *Clock Race to 60 Minutes* after the 60th day. (See page 43.)

- Many children like to "Celebrate the Hour" as they finally accumulate 60 minutes. In doing so, children rise at the 59th minute of every hour and watch the second hand make its journey to change the time to 60 minutes or a new hour. There is always applause for the new hour and then children are seated to wait again for the next hour to come. On that day, teachers add the short hand to the bulletin board Clock.

Catch the classroom clock when a new hour is just about to begin.

An alarm clock will remind everyone to notice the new hour on the wall clock.

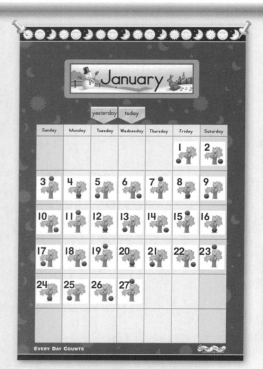

Every Day Calendar

Birthday Data

2 7 straws

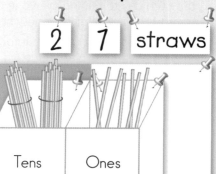

Daily Depositor

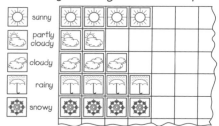

Graph

8 8

Clock

12:00 A.M.

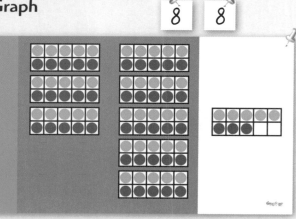

| 71 | 72 | 73 | 74 | 75 | 76 | 77 | 78 | 79 | 80 | 81 | 82 | 83 | 84 | 85 | 86 | 87 | 88 |

Counting Tape and Ten Grids

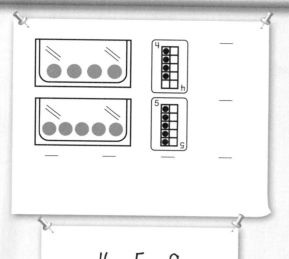

$$4 + 5 = 9$$

Number Builder

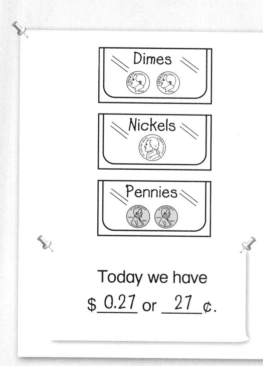

Dimes

Nickels

Pennies

Today we have
$ _0.27_ or _27_ ¢.

Coin Counter

In January, the Clock changes from showing the
number of school days in minutes to reflecting the
month's date in hours. The Coin Counter now has
a dime pocket along with the nickel and penny
pockets. The Daily Depositor provides another
place value model, and Number Builder presents
new strategies for addition and subtraction facts.
The Graph this month is another weather record
that might be used to compare fall and winter. The
Counting Tape and Ten Grids focus attention on
the question, "How many more until we have
100?" as Day 100 draws near.

CALENDAR

Concepts & Skills

- Recognize, analyze, and predict patterns
- Know the days of the week and months of the year in order
- Count with one-to-one correspondence
- Count on and count back
- Match quantities with numerals
- Read, compare, and order numbers to 31
- Solve problems using mental math
- Use position words to describe spatial orientation
- Interpret organized data

Ongoing Assessment

1. What is the first month of the year?
2. How would you describe this Calendar pattern with letters?
3. Describe the piece you see on the 2nd Saturday.

Author Notes

"This month's Calendar uses a ball that moves in space to investigate spatial or position language. *Left*, *right*, *over*, and *in front of* are among the position words that the children will use to describe this ABCD pattern. Throughout the month, provide the children with opportunities to explore these positions with their bodies."

Daily Routine

- Add a Calendar Piece daily.
- Twice a week discuss the pattern, encouraging children to use position vocabulary.

DISCUSSION

For the Beginning of the Month

Ask the class to point out the Birthday Package that matches the month written above the Calendar. Have the class name all the months in order, beginning with the January Package. Begin again with January, stopping with a clap on this month. Note that January is the first month of the new year. After reminding everyone of this year's new number, let children practice reading and writing it.

Move the January and July Packages near the Calendar and have children help you place the tags on the appropriate days.

For Throughout the Month

Look for the similarities and differences among the Calendar Pieces. As the children notice the different positions of the ball, elicit their descriptions of where the ball is located. You may hear language such as "next to the tree", "on top of the tree" and "in front of the tree." Throughout the month also introduce them to *left*, *right*, *over* and *in front of*, if the terms do not evolve from class discussions.

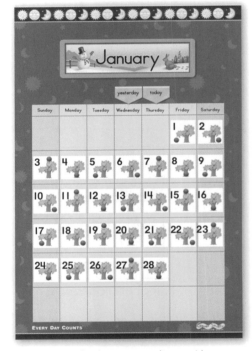

The January Calendar uses an oak tree with a ball that moves in space. The ball is seen to the left of the tree, to the right of the tree, over the tree, and in front of the tree, creating an ABCD pattern.

The ball is on the ground most of the time.

The ball is on the ground 3 days in a row, then it goes up to the top.

It's an ABCDABCD pattern.

It goes left, right, top, bottom, left, right, top, bottom.

Use body motions such as hand out to the left, hand out to the right, hand over the head, and hand, in front of the body to help children experience these positions.

To Sum Up

On one of the last days of January, ask children to look for patterns to share with the class.

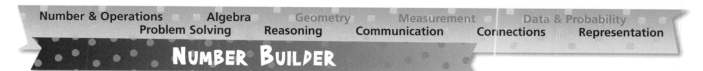

NUMBER BUILDER

Concepts & Skills

- Understand the processes of addition and subtraction
- Use the language of addition and subtraction
- Understand part and whole relationships for "doubles" and "doubles + 1"
- Develop strategies for addition and subtraction of "doubles" and "doubles + 1"
- See patterns in addition and subtraction
- Use symbolic notation to record addition and subtraction

Ongoing Assessment

1. What is a "double?" Tell me a "doubles" fact.
2. What is a neighbors or a "double + 1" problem? Tell me a neighbors fact.
3. How can you use a "doubles" fact to help you find 3 + 4?

Materials for January

Ten Grid Cards or TR8

Author Notes

"When children add numbers, they often relate one problem to another. For example, you might hear, "I know that 4 and 4 is 8 and 1 more makes 9." With this in mind, January's Number Builder encourages children to look at adding "doubles" (such as 4 and 4) and "neighbors" (such as 4 and 5 or 4 and 3).

Instead of focusing on one quantity for the entire month, January's Number Builder will add one counter a day for twelve days. During these 12 days the children will look at "doubles" facts when even quantities are split between the two pockets, and "doubles + 1" or "neighbors" facts for the odd quantities. For example, one day 8 counters will be shown as 4 and 4. The next day that changes to 5 and 4, illustrating the relationship between the doubles fact and the doubles + 1 fact. Children see that 4 and 5 are just 8 plus one more, or 9."

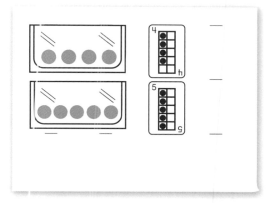

"Yesterday we had a double with 4 and 4. This is a double + 1 and we have 9."

Daily Routine

- **On the first of twelve days**, place one counter in the top pocket and hang a Ten Grid Card (TR8) for *1* to show the 1 and 0 combination.
- On the second day, add a new counter to the bottom pocket so that a double (1 and 1) appears.
- On the third day, the counter can be put in either pocket, changing the doubles to a doubles + 1 or neighbors problem.

- On the fourth day, even up the two groups to create the next double, and so on, through the 12th day.
- Each day after placing a counter in a pocket, create a picture record of the day's double or double + 1 by placing the appropriate Ten Grid Card adjacent to the pockets.
- Have the class tell what they see. Let children offer an addition or subtraction story to go with the counters appearing in the pockets.
- Record one story each day with words and with a number sentence on a paper strip.

DISCUSSION

For the Beginning of the Month

On the seventh day, 3 + 4, 4 + 3, 7 − 4, or 7 − 3 might be recorded. A discussion similar to the following might occur in your classroom.

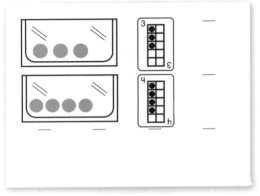

"Do you see the double inside of 3 and 4?"

Teacher: Did we build a double or a neighbor problem yesterday?

Class: Double.

Teacher: How do you know?

Child: We added the same number to itself. We added 2 threes.

Teacher: If we add one more today, what will our Ten Grid Cards show?

Class: 3 and 4.

Teacher: How might we add these neighbor numbers together?

Child: We could count 3, 4, 5, 6, 7.

Teacher: Could we look at yesterday's double to help us?

Child: Yes, 3 plus 3 equals 6 and 1 more is 7.

Teacher: Do you see that double inside of 3 and 4? Let's add these numbers again. (3 and 3 is 6 and one more is 7, so 3 and 4 is 7.) This is one way that we can think about adding these numbers.

DISCUSSION

For After the Twelfth Day

For the last two weeks in January, play a version of *Make the Sum* where two sets of the 1–6 Ten Grid Cards are placed faceup on the background mat and the children search for doubles or neighbors combinations. Or play *Make a Match* with the 1–6 Ten Grid Cards placed facedown and turned over two at a time in search of doubles and neighbors. If a match is found the child states the sum before removing the pair.

Number Sense To involve the class in discussion about strategies for adding doubles and neighbors, and to focus on the relationship of addition to subtraction, you might pose the following questions.

- Is this a double? Why?
- Is your answer to a doubles problem odd or even? How do you know? Will this always be true? (It is always even, since each counter or dot has a partner.)
- Tell us everything that you know about number neighbors.

- Will the answer to a neighbors problem be odd or even? Will this always happen whenever you add neighbors? (It will always be odd since there is one counter or dot without a partner.)

HELPFUL HINT

- Some teachers like to use doubles and doubles + 1 concentration as an independent activity to reinforce this concept. Ten Grid Cards are placed facedown in five rows of eight. Players take turns turning over two cards. If the cards show a double or a double + 1, the child states the addition and keeps the cards. If a double or double + 1 cannot be made, the cards are turned facedown and the next player takes a turn. The player with the most cards at the end of play wins.

Number & Operations	Algebra	Geometry	Measurement	Data & Probability
Problem Solving	Reasoning	Communication	Connections	Representation

DAILY DEPOSITOR

Concepts & Skills

- Count with one-to-one correspondence
- Match quantities and numerals
- Read numerals and compare quantities to 31
- Group and count by tens
- Understand place value

Materials for January

31 coffee stirrers, craft sticks, or straws; 3 rubber bands; 2 Depositor Boxes labeled tens and ones

Author Notes

"The items collected in the Daily Depositor vary from month to month in order to help children see the quantities 1 to 31 organized into tens and ones in different ways. This month straws are collected and bundled into tens with rubber bands.

Starting a fresh collection on the first of each month provides repeated opportunities for children to practice the counting sequence to 31 with one-to-one correspondence. It also provides opportunities for them to group and count objects by tens and ones and to learn to read and write these numbers with understanding. When children experience the teen numbers as "1 ten and one," "1 ten and two," and so on, it is easier to see how to write them without reversals."

Ongoing Assessment

1. Who can write a number sentence for 19 to show the ten and the ones?
2. How could you show 1 group of ten and 10 extra ones?
3. How many groups of ten are there in 23?

1 6 straws

Tens   Ones

Daily Routine

- Each day have a child place a straw in the box on the ones side of the Depositor. On Mondays, add two extras for Saturday and Sunday so the total is always the same as the day's date.
- Whenever ten straws accumulate, bundle them with a rubber band and move the bundle to the tens box on the tens side of the Depositor.
- Record the day's total above the boxes. Have children say the number of groups of ten and the number of ones as you write the numeral.

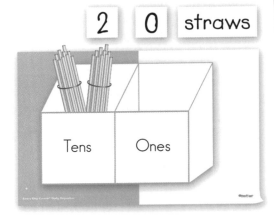

DISCUSSION

For Throughout the Month

The following discussion might occur in your classroom on January 20.

Sample Dialogue

Teacher: Today, you have said that we have 20 straws, since yesterday we had 19 and one more is 20. Is that right?

Child: We have 1 group of ten and 10 extra ones. That's 20.

Teacher: Do we have enough to make another group of ten?

Class: Yes, we can make a bundle of ten.

Teacher: Where is our special place for groups of ten?

Class: On the blue side.

Teacher: Now we have two groups of ten. Is that still the same as 1 group of ten and 10 extra ones?

Child: It is all 20.

Teacher: So, how can we show 20? (You may want to take the straws out of the Depositor to help count 20 in a variety of ways).

Child: We could have 2 groups of ten.

Child: We could have a pile of twenty straws.

Child: We could have 1 group of ten and 10 extra ones.

Teacher: Good thinking. It's all 20. How do we show it on our Depositor?

Class: 2 groups of ten and no leftovers.

Two ways to show 20.

HELPFUL HINT

- *Pick Up Sticks* On the last day of the month, the 31 straws can be removed from the Depositor and used to introduce a two-person game that involves looking for a pattern and using a strategy. Set out six straws. Take turns picking up one or two straws each time. The child who takes the last straw wins. Play three or four times. Ask everyone whether they think it's best to have the first or second turn. Suggest they try out their ideas by playing the game at home using toothpicks or pennies. Maybe they can figure out a way to win every time. When they find the game predictable, suggest they start with seven or eight straws. Can they use the same pattern to help them plan their moves to win?

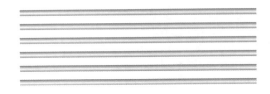

Play Pick Up Sticks

COUNTING TAPE AND TEN GRIDS

Concepts & Skills

- Develop number sense
- Group and count by tens, fives, and ones
- Understand place value
- See numbers 6–9 as a group of five and ones
- Compare and order quantities
- Use number patterns to add and subtract 10
- Use the language of duration

Daily Routine

- Continue to add 1 square and 1 dot each day.

DISCUSSION

For During the Month

| 73 | 74 | 75 | 76 | 77 | 78 | 79 | 80 | 81 | 82 | 83 | 84 | 85 | 86 |

Mental Math On days when 6 to 9 dots appear on the incomplete Ten Grid, continue to have children practice "pulling out the fives" to solve addition problems.

- How many dots would we have if we had two groups of 6?
- Two groups of 7?
- Can you tell us how you can use the five blue dots to figure this out?

With Day 100 approaching, the class can also consider special questions.

- How many more school days until this special day arrives?
- Can our color pattern on the Counting Tape help you figure this out?
- How many more full tens and extra ones do we need on our Ten Grids to make 100?
- How can you figure this out? What other ways could we find out?

The same strategy of "counting up" to the nearest ten and then counting on by tens can be used in both situations, and will be useful in figuring correct change and in doing mental addition and subtraction.

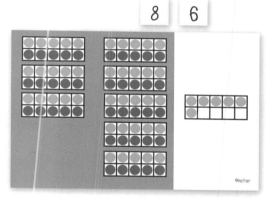

"How many more school days until Day 100?"

HELPFUL HINT

- If you'd like each child to bring in a collection of 100 things to help celebrate the one hundredth day of school, it is a good idea to brainstorm ideas for collections a few weeks ahead of time. Parents are usually very willing to support such a project if they know about it ahead of time. Let children know you wouldn't want them to risk having anything of personal value lost, stolen, or broken, so they shouldn't bring in toys, money, or collections they would be upset over losing. Ask children to group or organize their objects into tens so that everyone will be able to see the 10 tens in their hundred.

COIN COUNTER

Concepts & Skills

- Recognize the penny, nickel, and dime
- Know the value of each coin and coin equivalencies
- Count by tens, fives, and ones
- Determine the value of a collection of coins
- Use mental math to figure change
- Record money amounts using both the dollar sign with decimal point and the cent sign
- Problem solve with coins

Ongoing Assessment

1. How many coins do we have in our Coin Counter today?
2. A dime and four pennies is equal to how many cents?
3. How much is the money in our Coin Counter worth altogether?

Materials for January

Another clear pocket, labeled "dimes"; Dime Demonstration Card; Dime Coin Cards (TR22) or real dimes

Daily Routine

- The first day, catch up to the day's date by placing one penny at a time into the penny pocket for each day up to the present one. From this day on, add a penny a day. On Mondays, add pennies for Saturday and Sunday as well.
- Whenever 5 pennies accumulate, take them out and trade them for a nickel to put into the nickel pocket.
- When the next penny is added, model counting the nickel as five, and count on one more.
- When the second nickel is earned on the tenth, trade both nickels in for a dime and place it in the dime pocket.
- Throughout the month, continue trading for nickels and dimes whenever possible. Count each day's total by tens and ones or by tens, fives, and ones. For example, on January 19, children would count, "10, 15 (clap), 16, 17, 18, 19."
- Record the total cents below the Coin Counter in both the dollar sign with decimal point and the cent sign forms.
- Discuss once a week.

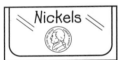

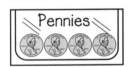

DISCUSSION

For the Beginning of the Month

As early in the month as possible, introduce the dime . Identify its value as 10¢. Add the large Dime Demo Coin to the display of the nickel and penny Demo Coins next to the Coin Counter. Pass out a dime to each child. Ask children to look at the dime to find some things that make it different from the nickel and the penny. Their observations may give you the opportunity to tell them a little bit about Franklin Roosevelt and the torch of liberty between sprigs of laurel and oak.

Today we have
$ _0.19_ or _19_ ¢.

"We have 10, 15 (clap), 16, 17, 18, 19 cents."

For Later in the Month

Mental Math Asking some of the following questions during the month may help develop some children's mental math skills. Invite children to suggest store problems of their own as well.

- How many days until we have 20¢? 30¢?

- How many pennies can you get for 2 nickels? 3 nickels?

- What coins do you think will be in the Counter on the 8th? On the 11th? On the 15th? On the 17th? On the 20th?

- If you were to take today's money from the Coin Counter to the store, would you have enough to buy something that costs 10¢? 15¢? 25¢?

- If you were to buy candy for 6¢, how much would you have left? What if you bought a small eraser for 16¢ instead?

Introduce the dime.

HELPFUL HINTS

- A collection of objects labeled with prices from 5¢ to 40¢ can make the store problems more real to children.

- When Barbara Garcia jingles her coin purse that holds dimes, nickels, and/or pennies, some first graders in Portland, Oregon, are eager to suggest possible solutions to the open-ended problems she poses. "I have 3 coins in my purse. How many cents could they be worth?" Or she poses the opposite situation, "I have 13¢. What coins could be in this purse?"

- Noting the children's suggestions by drawing coins in rows on a large piece of paper may help them to see the usefulness of making a list to keep track of all the possibilities when pursuing open-ended problems. The arrangements make it easier to see that one child's suggestion of 1 nickel and 8 pennies is the same as another's suggestion of 5 pennies, 1 nickel, and 3 more pennies.

- ▦ This is an excellent opportunity to let children experiment with calculators. Discuss how to add on a calculator, and allow children to confirm the cost of their purchases.

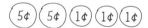

"I think the last two are the same. They both use one nickel and pennies."

Number & Operations	Algebra	Geometry	Measurement	Data & Probability
Problem Solving	Reasoning	Communication	Connections	Representation

CLOCK

Concepts & Skills

- Experience duration
- Understand analog and digital clocks
- Learn how many minutes are in an hour
- Count by fives and ones
- Read the minute and hour hands

Materials for the Rest of the Year

Clock with minute and hour hand attached; A.M./P.M. Chart (TR13)

Ongoing Assessment

1. (Show Clock set to 8:00.) What time is it on this Clock?
2. Set the Clock to 11:00.
3. If it is 2:00 now, what time will it be one hour from now?

Author Notes

"For the first 60 days of school, the Clock had only a minute hand which moved forward one minute per day. The children practiced counting by fives and ones and reading the minutes past any hour. Now in January, the focus switches to the shorter hour hand that is added to the bulletin board Clock. The Clock is used to show each of the 24 hours in a day as the Clock hands move ahead one hour on each of the first 24 days in January. By the time children have watched the minute hand advance through 60 minutes 24 times, they will begin to see the relationship between the long minute hand going around once and the short hour hand advancing just one hour."

Daily Routine

- As early in January as possible, update the Clock to the present day's date. Begin with the hands of the Clock pointing straight up, showing 12:00 midnight.
- Each day from then on, advance the Clock ahead one hour, reading the times at each 5-minute interval. On Mondays, add hours for Saturday and Sunday.
- Record an activity that would take place at that hour of the day on the A.M./P.M. Chart (TR13).
- **On the 13th,** advance to 1:00 P.M., on the 14th, to 2:00 P.M., and so on, until returning to 12:00 midnight on January 24.
- Put the Clock aside after January 24.

DISCUSSION

For the First Day

Explain to the children that each new day begins at 12:00 midnight in the middle of the night.

- Since 12:00 A.M. happens in the middle of the night, what should I write on our A.M./P.M. Chart that we were doing at 12:00 A.M.? (sleeping, most likely)
- Who would like to count with me by fives as I move the minute hand all the way around the clock? (12:05, 12:10, 12:15 . . .)
- (after reaching 1:00) How many minutes just went by on our Clock?
- What happened to the hour hand as the minute hand moved?
- How many hours just went by on our Clock?
- What should I write that we were doing at 1:00 A.M., just one hour after midnight?

For Later in the Month

On the 11th, take a moment for a brief discussion when the classroom clock also shows 11:00 A.M. On the 12th, stop at 12:00 noon and point out the change from A.M. to P.M. Involve children with discussion questions such as those that follow.

- What time does our classroom clock show?
- What time was it 1 hour ago? What were we doing 1 hour ago?
- What were we doing 2 hours ago? 3 hours ago?
- What time will it be 1 hour from now? 2 hours from now?

"What were we doing at midnight?"

	☽☆	☀
12 A.M.	sleep	
1 A.M.	sleep	
2 A.M.	sleep	
3 A.M.	sleep	
4 A.M.	sleep	
5 A.M.	sleep	
6 A.M.	sleep	
7 A.M.	sleep	
8 A.M.		breakfast
9 A.M.		
10 A.M.		
11 A.M.		
12 P.M.		
1 P.M.		
2 P.M.		
3 P.M.		
4 P.M.		
5 P.M.		
6 P.M.		
7 P.M.		
8 P.M.		
9 P.M.		
10 P.M.		
11 P.M.		

Number & Operations   Algebra   Geometry   Measurement   **Data & Probability**
Problem Solving   **Reasoning**   **Communication**   **Connections**   **Representation**

GRAPH

Concepts & Skills

- Collect and record data on a graph over time
- Read and interpret data on a picture or bar graph
- Count and compare small quantities

Materials for January

Graph paper (TR15), Weather Markers (TR16), October Weather Graph

Author Notes

"Graphing the weather again this month allows the class the opportunity to compare the kinds of weather that occurred in your area in the fall with the weather that occurs in the winter."

Daily Routine

- As in October, have the class look outside at the same time each day and decide what the weather is like.
- Have a volunteer attach the appropriate weather symbol to the Graph.
- Discuss the accumulating data once a week.

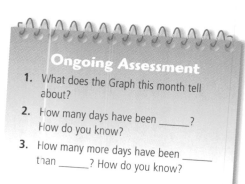

Ongoing Assessment

1. What does the Graph this month tell about?

2. How many days have been _____? How do you know?

3. How many more days have been _____ than _____? How do you know?

DISCUSSION

For the First Day

Have children participate in setting up a Graph that has the same headings in the same order as the October Weather Graph so it will be easy to compare the information on the two graphs. With the October Graph in view, let them tell you how to label the new January Graph. Place the first day's Weather Marker on the Graph.

For During the Month

At various points in the month, compare January's Graph to October's.

- Look at two Graphs. Who thinks there will be more sunny days in January than in October? Fewer sunny days? The same number?
- So far does it look like we will have more snowy days in January than we did in October?

HELPFUL HINT

- If you live in an area where the winter weather is similar to the fall weather, it might be fun to graph the winter weather of another part of the country in addition to your own. Perhaps a city could be chosen where friends or relatives of class members live who could correspond with the class or help set up correspondence with another first grade class in that area.

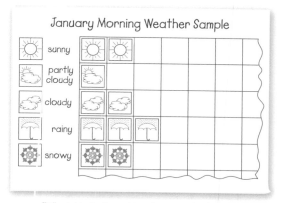

January Morning Weather Sample

sunny / partly cloudy / cloudy / rainy / snowy

"What kind of weather have we had most often so far?"

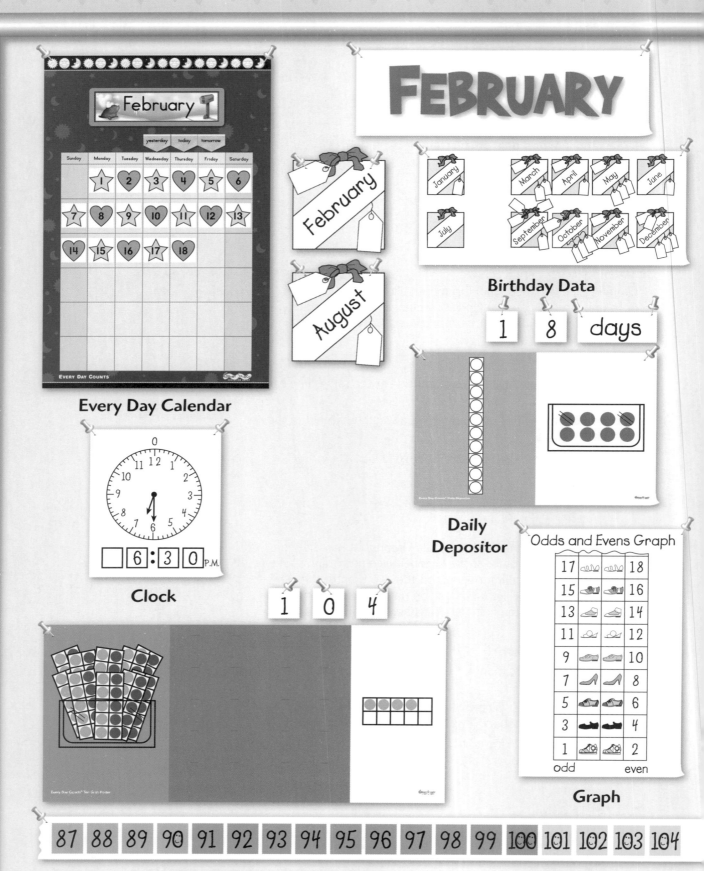

FEBRUARY

February

yesterday today tomorrow

Sunday	Monday	Tuesday	Wednesday	Thursday	Friday	Saturday
	1	2	3	4	5	6
7	8	9	10	11	12	13
14	15	16	17	18		

EVERY DAY COUNTS

Every Day Calendar

February

August

January March April May June

July September October November December

Birthday Data

1 8 days

Daily Depositor

Clock

6 : 3 0 P.M.

1 0 4

Odds and Evens Graph

17			18
15			16
13			14
11			12
9			10
7			8
5			6
3			4
1			2
odd			even

Graph

| 87 | 88 | 89 | 90 | 91 | 92 | 93 | 94 | 95 | 96 | 97 | 98 | 99 | 100 | 101 | 102 | 103 | 104 |

Counting Tape and Ten Grids

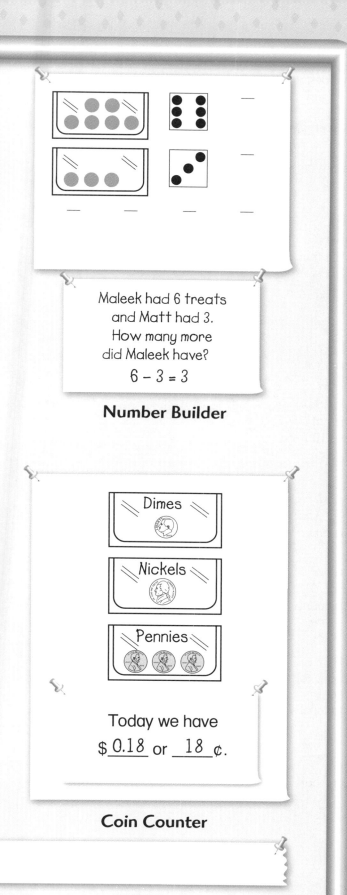

Maleek had 6 treats
and Matt had 3.
How many more
did Maleek have?
6 – 3 = 3

Number Builder

Today we have
$ 0.18 or 18 ¢.

Coin Counter

FEBRUARY ELEMENTS

February brings excitement as the 100th day of school arrives. This month the Counting Tape and Ten Grids focus on this special day when the hundreds place makes its debut. The hands of the Clock will move ahead one half hour each day, providing practice reading the hour and minute hands. The Calendar presents an odd and even color pattern. Fittingly, we add to the Coin Counter this month a pocket for quarters with George Washington's image. The Daily Depositor continues and Number Builder focuses on sums of 9. The Graph in February gives attention to odd and even numbers and counting by twos; a picture of a shoe is added each day of the month, forming even pairs every other day. Children will begin to see the connection between the odds and evens on the Graph and the pattern on the Calendar.

CELEBRATING THE 100TH DAY OF SCHOOL

One hundred is a special number in our numeration system. It provides a cornerstone for understanding the base ten system and higher numbers. For this reason, plan to set aside some time to do a few special activities on the 100th day of school. You might choose from the following suggestions or create several of your own.

Children's Collections of 100 Objects: On Day 100, the collections can be displayed, and children can consider questions similar to those that follow.

- How many collections of 100 have been brought in?

- How could we find out how many things there are altogether? (If you count by hundreds, when the class reaches ten 100s, explain that ten 100s make 1000.)

- Which collections do you think would form the longest lines if the items were laid out end to end? Which do you think weighs the most? Why do you think so? How could we find out?

How Far Will 100 Steps Take Us? Sometime during the day on the way to the lunchroom or gym have the class guess how far 100 giant steps will take them. Let a few at a time go ahead, counting their steps as they go. Were their guesses too far, just about right, or too near?

Which Bag Has 100? Put some individually wrapped candies in each of three resealable plastic bags. Make sure that one bag holds exactly 100. Invite children to guess: Which bag holds 100, Bag A, B, or C? It might be fun to tally or graph the guesses. Then assign two or three volunteers to each collection. Have them group the contents of their bag into tens so the whole class can see and count out the totals. Are the results surprising to some? Did more children choose the bag of 100 when making their guesses or did more people choose one of the other bags? Divide the collections among class members and enjoy!

One Hundred? Prove It! Pair up children and pass out containers of different objects such as crayons, paper clips, small cubes, buttons, bread tags, or small rocks. Ask the partners to decide on a way to count out and show 100 items so that others will be able to easily check their work. Let children view one another's displays and talk about some of the different ways the objects have been organized.

Creating Hundredth Day Designs: Let children use a variety of crayons to shade 100 squares on Blank Hundred Charts (TR21). Some will choose to create abstract designs or patterns. Others will make representational pictures. After displaying them a while, gather them into a book. Children's responses to "What do you see in this design?" can be recorded on the page opposite each design.

What Can We Do 100 Times? Some teachers break up the day with short periods of exercise. Children enjoy seeing if they can do 10 sets of 10 jumping jacks, for example, or march in place 100 steps.

LEAP YEAR

If it is a leap year or if you have a child with a February 29th birthday, you might want to mention that February is unique, since it gets an extra day every 4 years (except centenary years not divisible by 400).

CALENDAR

Concepts & Skills

- Recognize, analyze, and predict patterns
- Know the days of the week and months of the year in order
- Find tomorrow on the calendar
- Count with one-to-one correspondence to 28 or 29
- Read, compare, and order numbers to 28 or 29
- Count on and count back
- Match quantities with numerals
- Understand odd and even numbers and pairs
- Solve problems and use mental math
- Interpret organized data

Ongoing Assessment

1. How many birthdays do we have in February and August together?
2. What color or shape will we get on February 14?
3. Is 6 even or odd? Show us how you know.

Materials for the Rest of the Year

Tomorrow Marker

Daily Routine

- Add a Calendar Piece daily.
- Introduce the Tomorrow Arrow Marker this month. Have a volunteer name tomorrow's date after telling the current day's date.
- Guide discussions to encourage children to distinguish odd and even and understand pairs.

DISCUSSION

For the Beginning of the Month

Ask the class to point out the Birthday Package that matches the month written above the Calendar. Have the class name all the months in order. Then begin again with January, stopping with a clap on February. Note that February is the second month of the new year.

Invite children to predict where the February birthdays and the August half-year "unbirthdays" will appear on the Calendar and mark them with the tags taken from the Birthday Packages.

Problem Solving Fit in a question or two about the birthday data at transition times or when lining up for recess or lunch.

- Can you find 2 months that have 5 birthdays in all?
- Can you find 2 Birthday Packages that have the same number of tags and together have 6?
- Can you find 2 months where one Package has 4 more than the other?

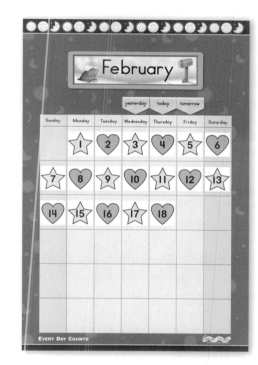

The February Calendar Pieces create an ABAB pattern with blue stars and red hearts.

For the Second Week

Algebraic Thinking There are some special days coming up this month. Involve children in predicting their colors and where they will fall on the Calendar, using the ABAB pattern. Go ahead and place the Calendar Pieces for these days on the Calendar.

- Valentine's Day is February 14. What color do you think it will be? How did you get your answer?

- Abraham Lincoln's birthday is February 12. Will the piece used on his birthday be the same color as the one on Valentine's Day? How did you decide?

- George Washington's birthday is February 22. What color will this piece be? How do you know this?

- Presidents' Day, the third Monday of this month, is a national holiday honoring both Presidents' birthdays. Where is the third Monday going to be and what color will it be?

Once the pattern has been revealed, let children suggest and try several interpretations of the basic ABAB pattern within one discussion period. Encourage them to look at color, the shapes with curved sides and straight sides, and the numbers. At other times, let children use various materials to create an ABAB pattern of their own, looking at size, position, shape, and color. You might ask the class to keep an eye out for ABAB patterns around the school, home, and neighborhood and ask them to tell you when they find one.

To Sum Up

Odd and Even The alternating color pattern will make the pattern of odd and even numbers stand out. By slightly rotating every two Calendar Pieces toward each other, overlapping at the bottom, a visual representation of odd and even is created with even quantities showing pairs and odd quantities showing a leftover unpaired piece.

With the month's Calendar Pieces still in place, you may choose to explore the counting pattern of twos by taking the first piece off, leaving the second piece on, taking the third piece off, and so on. This off, on, off, on, off, on pattern leaves red hearts in a counting pattern of twos.

Algebraic Thinking The following questions might be helpful to encourage searching for number patterns.

- What do you notice about the pieces that are remaining?
- What do you add to 2 to get to 4? To 4 to get to 6? To 6 to get to 8?
- Is this a pattern? Why?
- What keeps happening over and over? (adding two)
- Does this number pattern keep growing?

You might want to show this number pattern by setting out some rows of cubes that increase by two. The 1st row would include 2 cubes, the 2nd row would have 4 cubes, the 3rd row would have 6 cubes, and so on. A pictorial record of the cubes and a written record of the children's observations might be an option to elicit further discussion.

"What do you notice about these pieces?"

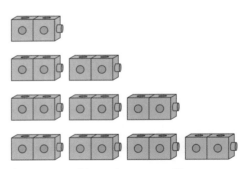

"How many will be in the next row?"

HELPFUL HINTS

- Since the pattern for even numbers is highlighted on the Calendar this month, involve children in brainstorming a list of things that come in twos. Then, using the list, everyone can suggest story problems that involve counting by twos. For example, 4 pairs of boots would go on how many feet?

- The Calendar Pieces can be used to interest children in exploring spatial relationships. To get children looking for symmetry in two-dimensional shapes, begin with the Heart Calendar Piece. Demonstrate how folding it down the center can be a test for `symmetry`. If the two halves are congruent (the same size and the same shape), matching up exactly, the fold is a line of symmetry. Let them experiment with the star pieces to see if they can fold them into matching congruent halves and find the lines of symmetry.

- If you found the Draw and Replace probability experiment in October instructive, or if you didn't get a chance to do it, this month's Calendar Pieces offer children the opportunity to conduct an experiment with two equally likely outcomes. See October (page 36) for details.

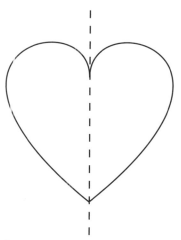

"A line of symmetry makes two halves that are exactly the same."

Number & Operations	Algebra	Geometry	Measurement	Data & Probability
Problem Solving	Reasoning	Communication	Connections	Representation

NUMBER BUILDER

Concepts & Skills

- Understand addition and subtraction
- Use the language of addition and subtraction (take away and comparison)
- Discuss part and whole relationships for 9
- See patterns in addition and subtraction
- Use symbolic notation to record addition and subtraction
- Match quantities and numerals
- Share number stories

Ongoing Assessment

1. How much more is 6 than 3?
2. List all of the ways that we can make 9.
3. Can you share an adding, take away, or comparing story with us?

Author Notes

"This month the Number Builder displays the quantity of 9 for the children to see and talk about. As in September, the focus of Number Builder for the first two weeks of this month is to help children explore addition, take-away subtraction, and comparison story problems as they relate to the various arrangements of 9 appearing in the two pockets. For the last two weeks of the month we again suggest versions of *Make the Sum* and *Make a Match*."

Daily Routine

- Two or three days a week have volunteers divide 9 counters between the two pockets and clip the corresponding Domino Halves to the right side of the mat.
- Invite children to tell addition or subtraction stories that relate to the display of counters.
- Record one story with words and with a number sentence.
- When all the combinations for 9 have been explored, finish the month playing *Make the Sum* and *Make a Match*.

DISCUSSION

For During the Month

Addition and Subtraction Concepts Number Builder is visited two to three times a week with a brief discussion on some days followed by more extensive discussions on other days. Here are some questions you might ask the children to promote understanding of adding and subtracting and their inverse relationship.

- Who has a story about adding with these counters to share with us? A take-away story? A comparing story?
- We just wrote $9 - 6 = 3$ to describe our story. Where did the 9 come from? What does the 6 represent?
- What do we need to add to 6 to get to 9?
- How much more than 6 is 9?
- How many different ways can we find to make 9?
- How many different take-away number sentences can we write to match our counters?
- How can you figure out the answer for $9 - 2$? $9 - 3$?

Maleek had 9 treats
and Matt had 6.
How many more
did Maleek have?
$9 - 6 = 3$

For Later in the Month

Addition Facts For the last two weeks of the month, you may choose to play a version of *Make the Sum* where all Domino Halves are placed faceup on the background mat and the children search for combinations for 9. Or invite a volunteer to draw one Domino Card, represent it with counters in one pocket, and clip it onto the mat. Domino Cards are then drawn in search of the one card that is needed as an addend to make 9.

Finally, *Make a Match*, a memory game where Domino Cards are placed facedown and turned over two at a time in search of combinations for 9, is another option.

On the last day of the month, create permanent Domino Cards for combinations for 9 to add to your classroom collection.

HELPFUL HINT

- Continue to use the Domino Cards that you have made for 5, 6, 7, 8, and 9 for review. They can be sorted by +0, +1, +2, +3, +4, and doubles for variety when playing *Quick as You Can*.

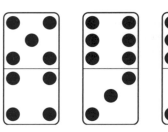

Use your Domino Cards to play *Quick as You Can*.

DAILY DEPOSITOR

Concepts & Skills

- Count with one-to-one correspondence
- Match quantities and numerals
- Compare quantities to 28 or 29
- Read numerals to 28 or 29
- Group and count by tens
- Understand place value

Materials for February

A collection of 29 disc-shaped counters; 4 strips of 1 × 10 circular arrays (TR19)

Author Notes

"This month in the Daily Depositor round counters are collected one per day on the ones side of the Depositor. On the tenth day of the month, the counters are traded for one strip of ten circles that is placed on the tens side of the Depositor. The number of tens and ones are displayed above the respective mats."

Daily Routine

- Each day of the month, have a volunteer place a counter in the pocket on the ones side of the Depositor. On Mondays, add counters for Saturday, Sunday, and Monday so the total is always the same as the day's date.
- Whenever 10 counters accumulate, trade them in for one strip of ten circles and place it on the tens side. You may choose to color the circles in the strips, making sure that all circles are the same color.
- Each day, record or display the total in tens and ones, or expanded notation.

DISCUSSION

For Throughout the Month

Place Value, Mental Math Continue to invite the children to verify the total amount represented in the Depositor in a variety of ways.

- How many tens and how many ones do we have today?
- Twenty-four is the same as how many tens and how many ones?
- Twenty-six is the same as twenty plus what?
- If I remove a strip of ten, how much is left in the Depositor?
- If I remove one counter how many counters are left?

Ongoing Assessment

1. (pointing to the 2 in the tens place) What does this 2 tell us? (pointing to the 4 in the ones place) What does this 4 tell us?

2. How many more days until we fill another strip of ten?

3. Which is greater 12 or 21? How do you know?

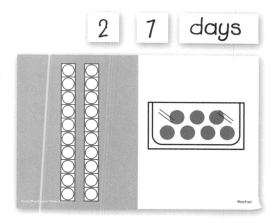

2 7 days

Sample Dialogue

Teacher: How many counters do we see in all today?

Child: There are 20. Yesterday we had 19 and 1 more is 20.

Teacher: What does our Depositor show us?

Child: We have 1 group of ten and extra ones.

Teacher: How many extra ones?

Child: We can count them. 1, 2, 3, 4, . . ., 10. We have ten.

Teacher: So, 1 group of ten and ten extra ones make 20. Do we have enough ones to make an equal trade for a strip of ten?

Child: Yes, we have ten ones.

Teacher: Is this an equal trade? Did we give ten and get ten? What does our Depositor show now?

Class: 2 groups of ten.

Teacher: Let's show this with numbers. We need a 2 for the 2 groups of ten and a 0 for the extra ones.

Number & Operations	Algebra	Geometry	Measurement	Data & Probability
Problem Solving	Reasoning	Communication	Connections	Representation

COUNTING TAPE AND TEN GRIDS

Concepts & Skills

- Develop number sense
- Count with one-to-one correspondence
- Group and count by tens, fives, and ones
- Understand place value
- Read three-digit numbers
- Compare and order quantities
- Count on and count back
- Use number patterns to add and subtract 10

Ongoing Assessment

1. How many groups of ten are in one hundred?
2. What number comes after 100?
3. How do we write the number one hundred five?

Materials for the Rest of the Year

A small plastic pocket for the hundreds place on the Ten Grids poster

| 92 | 93 | 94 | 95 | 96 | 97 | 98 | 99 | 100 | 101 | 102 | 103 | 104 |

Daily Routine

- Repeat the same sequence of colors used for the decades to 100 when putting up squares for days beyond 100.
- Until day 100, continue to consider the question, "How many more school days until Day 100?" using both the Counting Tape and the Ten Grids.
- After Day 100, ask questions that help children see the relationship between these large numbers and the smaller numbers from the beginning of the school year.

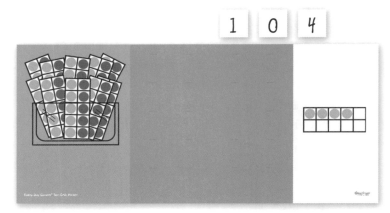

DISCUSSION

For the Hundredth Day of School

The hundredth day of school offers great opportunities for discussions about the Counting Tape and Ten Grids.

Sample Dialogue

Teacher: How many days have we been in school as of today? What comes after Day 99?

Class: One hundred.

Teacher: Yes, it is our 100th day of school, Day 100. Let's see how many complete groups of ten we have on the Counting Tape.

Teacher & Class: 1 ten to 10, 2 tens to 20, 3 tens to 30, 4 tens to 40, 5 tens to 50, 6 tens to 60, 7 tens to 70, 8 tens to 80, 9 tens to 90, and 10 tens to 100.

Teacher: Yes, 10 tens in 10 different colors. Remember how we wrote 80 with an 8 and a 0, meaning 8 tens and 0 ones, and how we wrote 90 with a 9 and a 0, meaning 9 tens and 0 ones? Watch as the pattern continues. Today I'm writing a 10 and a 0 to mean 10 tens and 0 ones. This number we read as 100 also means 10 tens. How do we usually read this number?

Class: One hundred.

Teacher: And how many groups of ten do we have?

Child: 10 tens.

Teacher: Yes. What do you think the next number will be?

Child: Two hundred.

Child: A million.

Child: One hundred and one.

Teacher: Keep thinking about it. We'll find out tomorrow (or the next school day). Now let's look at our Ten Grids. Can you count the dots by tens with me?

Class: 10, 20, 30, . . ., 100.

Teacher: Yes. Today we finally have 100. How many full 10 grids did it take to make 100? Let's count them.

Class: 1 ten, 2 tens, 3 tens, . . ., 10 tens.

Teacher: So 10 tens make 100 here too. Do you remember that a grid filled with 10 dots is special enough to be moved over to its own tens place? Well, when 10 Ten Grids become filled, the new 100 is special enough to get its own place too. We'll move all these grids with 100 dots on them to the hundreds place. What's left in the tens place?

Class: Nothing.

Teacher: Now what should I write under each place? How many complete hundreds do we have?

Class: 1.

MORE ▶

Teacher: Yes, so I'll write a 1 under the hundreds place to show we have just one hundred. How many filled tens do you see in the tens place?

Class: None.

Teacher: Yes, so I'll write a 0 under the tens place to show we have no extra tens. How many dots are on the empty grid attached to the ones place?

Class: None.

Teacher: So, I'll record a 0 under the ones place to show we have no extra ones. We can read 100 as, "One hundred, zero tens, and zero ones, or one hundred." Now let's all read it.

Class: One hundred, zero tens, and zero ones, or one hundred.

Teacher: We can also see that 100 means ten tens and no extra ones. I wonder how many dots we'll have all together on our next day of school when we add another dot? Think about it for a moment. We'll find out tomorrow (or the next school day).

For After the Hundredth Day of School

On Day 101, when the day's square is displayed, continue the discussion begun on Day 100. Focus on the number of completed tens making up 100, and the one additional day. Some will be surprised to find out that 101 follows 100. Discuss the numbers that appear on following days in the same way.

Also continue with discussions about the Ten Grids Poster similar to the one for Day 100, focusing on recording and naming the hundreds, tens, and ones. Occasionally name all the tens, including those within the hundred. Children can see 101 is 10 tens plus 1 at the same time that it is 1 hundred plus 1. Once a week take time to organize and count the dots in different ways.

HELPFUL HINTS

- If you have been attaching the optional yellow dot stickers to the zeros in 10, 20, . . ., 90 and decorating them with the face of Zero the Hero, you will want to make a special event of his appearing twice on Day 100. In Veronica Paracchini's primary classroom in Portland, Oregon, the children celebrated Zero the Hero Day on Day 100. They then decided that it should really be Zero the Hero Month since he kept reappearing day after day for 10 more school days. Nothing like this had happened before!

- Some teachers arrange to have Zero the Hero visit on Day 100. Wearing a bright yellow cape, decorated with the word Zero and numbers with zeros in them, Zero the Hero asks about the day's special activities and leaves behind zero-shaped cereal treats for everyone.

- Play *Collect 100*. Players will need 200 small counters and 20 ten cups or other containers to hold groups of ten counters. Partners take turns rolling a 4 to 9 number cube and collecting that number of counters. Whenever ten counters accumulate, they are placed in a cup. Players tell their totals before each turn. The first player to reach 100 by filling 10 ten cups wins.

- For more suggestions of activities celebrating Day 100, see page 86.

COIN COUNTER

Concepts & Skills

- Know the penny, nickel, dime, and quarter
- Know the value of each coin and coin equivalencies
- Count by tens, fives, and ones
- Determine the value of a collection of coins
- Use mental math, including figuring change
- Record money amounts using both the dollar sign with decimal point and the cent sign
- Solve problems with coins

Materials for the Rest of the Year

A clear pocket labeled *quarters*, the Quarter Demonstration Card, and copies of quarter Coin Cards (TR22) or real quarters

Author Notes

"In February, the Coin Counter introduces the quarter. As a penny a day is added to the Counter, children trade 2 dimes and a nickel for a quarter as well as 5 pennies for a nickel and 2 nickels for a dime. Counting out the total value of the coins each day children get practice in counting by tens, fives, and ones."

Daily Routine

- Add one penny on the first of the month as previously.
- Make trades when possible, and this month trade the 2 dimes and the nickel appearing on the 25th of the month for a quarter.
- Ask a variety of shopping problems that challenge children to use mental math and problem solving skills.

DISCUSSION

For February 25

Comparing Identify the quarter's value as 25¢. Add the Quarter Demo Coin and a quarter pocket to the Coin Counter display. Pass around three or four traditional quarters and three or four of the newer quarters representing the states so that each child can feel and briefly examine the real coins. Ask children to look at the quarters and the Large Demo Pictures of all the coins. How are the quarters similar to the other coins? How are they different?

They may mention that all the quarters have a man on one side, like the other coins, but that the backs are different. Their observations may give you the opportunity to tell them a little about George Washington, who served from 1789–1797 as the nation's first President. You could mention that the newer quarters will have different pictures on the backs and the older quarters have an eagle on the back. Explain that

Ongoing Assessment

1. Show me a dime, a nickel, and a penny. How many cents are these coins worth?
2. Two dimes and a nickel are how many cents?
3. What coins could we use to show _____ cents?

"How are quarters similar to other coins? How are they different?"

E pluribus unum means *out of many, one*, referring to the creation of the United States out of the several colonies. Following the discussion, collect the quarters and use a quarter in the Coin Counter to replace the two dimes and the nickel.

For During the Month

Mental Math Asking some of the following questions now and then during the month may help develop children's mental math skills. Sometimes invite children to suggest store problems of their own as well.

- How many coins are in our Counter?
- Can you think of a different group of coins we could use that would add up to the same amount?
- What coins do you think will be in our Counter on the 8th? On the 11th? On the 17th? On the 20th?
- If you were to take today's money from the Coin Counter to the store, would you have enough to buy something for 12¢? 15¢? 25¢? If so, would you get change? How much?

HELPFUL HINTS

- February is a most appropriate month for introducing the quarter. Some teachers note Washington's and Lincoln's birthdays on the Calendar by attaching a quarter or a Quarter Coin Card on February 22, a penny on February 12, or both coins on Presidents' Day. (See Calendar, page 88.)
- To give children experience with probability and to help them become familiar with the new state quarters, you might invite children to work with a partner to toss a state quarter ten times. Then they can trade for a different state quarter for the next ten tosses, and so on until each pair of children has tossed 100 times. They can keep track of results by crossing out numbers on two Hundred Charts (TR20), one for heads and one for tails or by tallying. Discuss whether end results are close to fifty and fifty.
- Continue to play the *Coin Collector* game, adding in dimes. (See December, p. 70.) Partners take turns tossing a 1–6 number cube and collecting that amount in pennies. Five pennies are traded for a nickel whenever possible, and two nickels are traded for a dime whenever possible. Players state their total amounts before each toss. The first player to trade two dimes and a nickel for a quarter is the winner.
- Reading and displaying a few picture books that describe the Revolutionary War period and George Washington's life may spark children's interest in American History.

Quarter Toss	
Heads	Tails
ЖЖ 5	ЖЖ 5
ЖЖ 10	ЖЖ 10
ЖЖ 15	ЖЖ 15
ЖЖ 20	ЖЖ 20
	‖

"It came up tails again. Now I have 22 tails."

CLOCK

Concepts & Skills

- Experience duration
- Understand analog and digital clocks
- Learn how many minutes are in an hour
- Count by fives and ones
- Read the minute and hour hands

Author Notes

"In February, the Clock will move ahead one half hour a day, and now the focus will be on reading the Clock at every half hour. On February 1, the Clock will be set to nine o'clock or any other preferred hour. Each day after that the Clock will move forward one half hour daily to help children to understand that a half hour is 30 minutes, to see the Clock at half hour intervals, and to continue to become more aware of the passage of time throughout the day."

Daily Routine

- As early in February as possible, set the Clock to 9 o'clock A.M. or a preferred hour.
- Each day from then on, slowly advance the hands of the Clock ahead one half hour. On Mondays, add half hours for Saturday and Sunday.
- Have the class read the time at each five-minute interval as the minute hand passes through the 30 minutes.
- Each day, record the new time shown on the Clock and identify an activity that would take place at this time on the A.M./P.M. Chart.

DISCUSSION

For the First Day

Clock Sense Begin with the hands of the Clock pointing to 9:00 A.M. or a preferred hour good for classroom discussion.

- What hour is the short hand pointing to? (9)
- How many minutes past zero has the long hand moved? (0)
- How do we read this time? (9 o'clock)
- Let's count by fives as I move the minute hand 30 minutes . . . Now where is the long hand pointing? (to the 6)
- What hour is the short hand pointing to now? (It's halfway between 9 and 10.)
- How do we read this time? (9:30)
- What do we usually do at 9:30 in the morning when we're in school?
- How many minutes are between 9:30 and 10:00?

Ongoing Assessment

1. How many minutes is half an hour?
2. (showing a Clock set to 4:30) What time does the Clock show?
3. Can you move the Clock hand from 10:30 forward 30 minutes? What time will it be?

9 A.M.		attendance
9:30 A.M.		Calendar
10 A.M.		reading
10:30 A.M.		recess
11 A.M.		writing
11:30 A.M.		music
12 P.M.	lunch	
12:30 P.M.	story time	
1 P.M.	math	
1:30 P.M.	science	
2 P.M.		
2:30 P.M.		
3 P.M.		
3:30 P.M.		
4 P.M.		
4:30 P.M.		
5 P.M.		
5:30 P.M.		
6 P.M.		
6:30 P.M.		
7 P.M.		
7:30 P.M.		

For Throughout the Month

Elapsed Time Try to catch the classroom clock at the time shown on the bulletin board Clock during the day and read the classroom clock. Point out the change from A.M. to P.M. as you pass 12:00 noon.

To develop understanding of duration, ask the class to determine what time it was one half hour ago and what was happening then. Also, ask what time it will be in one more half hour.

Here are some sample questions for discussion about half hours and elapsed time.

- What time does our Clock show today?
- What time was it yesterday on our bulletin board Clock?
- How many minutes did we count today to go from __ to __?
- What were we doing a half hour ago?
- We set the Clock to the hour or half hour each day. Can you tell me two other times that are a half hour apart?
- Why do you think we call 30 minutes a half hour?

Number & Operations • **Algebra** • **Geometry** • **Measurement** • **Data & Probability**
Problem Solving • **Reasoning** • **Communication** • **Connections** • **Representation**

GRAPH

Concepts & Skills

- Collect and record data on a graph over time
- Read and interpret data on a picture or bar graph
- Organize quantities into pairs
- Count by twos
- Recognize odd and even patterns

Materials for February

3 sheets of Graph paper (TR15), 29 shoe markers (TR16)

Author Notes

"This month the Graph will display odd and even quantities and encourage counting by twos. When one shoe picture is added each day, pairs form on the second, fourth, sixth, eighth, and so on, helping children see that an even number of objects can be broken into pairs. On the odd-numbered days, the collection of shoes shows an extra shoe with no partner."

Setup

Prepare the Graph by attaching three sheets of Graph paper to make a 4 by 15 grid.

Ongoing Assessment

1. What does "even number" mean?
2. Draw a picture of an odd number of flowers and show how you can tell it is an odd number.
3. Is 9 odd or even? How can you tell?

Daily Routine

- On the first of the month, add a picture of a shoe to the second square of the bottom row on the Graph. The next day add that shoe's partner to the adjacent square, the third square of the bottom row.

- Continue to add a shoe each day, forming a pair every 2 days. On Mondays, add shoes for Saturday, Sunday, and Monday.

- Ask the class to count all the shoes by twos, counting on the extra one on odd-numbered days. Ask if the day's number of shoes reveals an even "all paired up" arrangement or an odd arrangement showing an extra shoe with no partner.

- Record the total each day next to the last shoe.

DISCUSSION

For During the Month

Odds and Evens Once a week focus discussion on the emerging odd/ even pattern. Questions similar to these will foster conversation.

- How can you tell if the number is even or odd? What does it mean to be an odd or an even number?

- How many more days until the number of shoes will be even again? Odd again?

- Can we find a pattern in the even numbers we have written so far? In the odd numbers?

- If I mark the last day of February on the Graph with an X, can you look at the pattern and decide if the last day will be even or odd? How do you know?

- How many shoes will there be on the last day of the month?

HELPFUL HINTS

- Ask the class to look for connections between the ABAB patterns emerging on the Calendar and the Shoe Graph. You might want to occasionally have children represent the pairs of shoes with pairs of different-colored connecting cubes.

- Whenever the opportunity arises during the month, try counting quantities by twos instead of always by ones. For example, it might be fun to take attendance counting those present by twos. Is the total odd or even? If we pair up with partners today, will someone be left without a partner?

- One teacher at Newman School in New Orleans records the children's responses to, "What does it mean to be an odd number or an even number?" One child's comment, "Being an odd number is not having a partner to dance with," inspired the beginning of an illustrated odd-and-even book.

"Do we have an odd number or an even number of shoes today?"

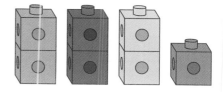

"Do we have an odd or even number of cubes?"

MARCH

Every Day Calendar

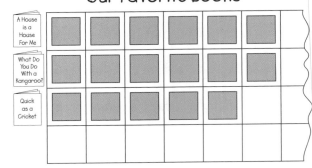

Birthday Data

Our Favorite Books

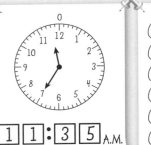

Clock

Graph

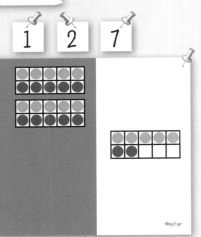

Measurement

| 110 | 111 | 112 | 113 | 114 | 115 | 116 | 117 | 118 | 119 | 120 | 121 | 122 | 123 | 124 | 125 | 126 | 127 |

Counting Tape and Ten Grids

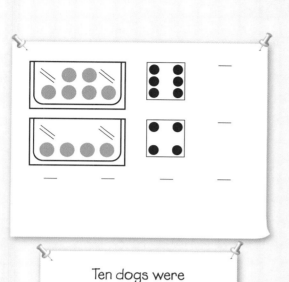

Ten dogs were
at the park
and 4 ran away.

10 − 4 = 6

Number Builder

Today we have
$ _0.31_ or _31_ ¢.

Coin Counter

Children see relationships and make connections
at different times. For example, while some can
see tens and ones on the Counting Tape from the
11th day of school, others may not make the
connection until several months later, and some
not until year's end. An attitude of joy at their
insights encourages even children with the least
sophisticated number sense to get involved.

This month the Counting Tape and Ten Grids
familiarize children with quantities above 100
while Number Builder focuses on sums for 10. The
Calendar exposes children to a growing pattern, in
which one large bear alternates with an increasing
number of small bears. The Coin Counter displays
several arrangements of coins equal to the day's
date in cents. The minute hand of the Clock this
month advances by 5 minutes a day.

The Graph is the highlight of March. The class
decides on a survey question, conducts a poll,
graphs part of the sample each day, and analyzes
the accumulating data. The class survey may
encourage some children to do polls of their own.

CALENDAR

Concepts & Skills

- Recognize, analyze, and predict patterns
- Know the days of the week and months of the year in order
- Count with one-to-one correspondence to 31
- Read, compare, and order numbers to 31
- Count on and count back
- Explore a growing pattern
- Solve problems using mental math
- Interpret organized data

Daily Routine

- Add a Calendar Piece a day.
- Explain that a new pattern is beginning to appear on the March Calendar and that it might not show up right away.
- Allow children to puzzle over the emerging pattern until several begin to see it.
- Help children see that a growing pattern is a different kind of pattern.

DISCUSSION

For the Beginning of the Month

Analyzing Data Point out that March is the third month of the year. Have children help you place Birthday Package tags on the Calendar as usual. Occasionally, ask children to figure how many days until the next birthday. How much older is one March birthday child than another? Listen to those willing to share how they came to their conclusions.

Counting, Comparing The lineup of Birthday Packages also continues to offer an ever-present invitation to compare, count, add, and subtract. A few examples of the kinds of questions that get children thinking follow.

- Are there more birthdays this month or during your birthday month?
- How many birthdays come in March and April? In April and May?
- How many months until your birthday month arrives?
- How many fewer birthdays are in January than in April?
- I see 2 months next to each other where the tags add up to 6 in all. Which 2 months could these be?

When there is more than one possible correct answer, acknowledge one solution, then ask for another.

The March Calendar Pieces create a growing pattern. One big bear alternates with a growing number of small bears in the pattern 1 big, 1 small, 1 big, 2 small, 1 big, 3 small, and so on.

For the Second Week in March

This month's Calendar investigation will provide a concrete experience with a growing pattern. Let children simply make observations about this month's pattern with the bears on the Calendar. The questions that follow will facilitate a discussion about the growing pattern.

Algebraic Thinking To recognize and explore a pattern that grows:

- What do you see happening with this month's pattern or is this a pattern? (Some children will not agree that this is a pattern.)
- Would someone like to point to each bear and say its size out loud?
- Let's say the size of the bears again and clap every time we come to a small bear. Does anyone notice anything about how many times we clapped?
- What do you notice about the number of small bears in between the big bears? (Children may see that we keep adding one more.)
- Did you know that a pattern is something that happens over and over again or repeats? What do you see that keeps repeating? This is called a growing pattern, since it grows by adding one, then adding one more, over and over again.

Continue to revisit this idea of a pattern that grows throughout the month. You may still have some children who are unsure of this thinking, but this concept will continually be revisited.

HELPFUL HINTS

- You may also want to focus on the number of bear ears in each group of small bears. If you choose to highlight the twos in this month's Calendar pattern, review the list created in February of things that come in twos, or brainstorm a new list.
- These suggestions can be used in story problems that encourage children to add by twos. For example:
  - How many wheels are on two bikes? Three bikes? Four bikes?
  - How many mittens are in one pair? Two pairs? Three pairs?
  - If I get two nickels for one dime, how many can I get for two dimes? Three dimes? Four dimes?
  - If I cut a muffin in half, I'd get two pieces. How many pieces will I get if I cut two muffins in half?
  - If it takes two people to turn one jump rope, how many people do we need to turn three ropes? Four ropes?

March Pattern

- The pattern is large bear, small bear, large bear, small bear, small bear.
- We keep getting more small bears.
- The big bears stay the same, but we keep adding a little bear.
- We add one more little bear each time.
- It is a growing pattern.
- The little bears go 1, 2, 3, 4, 5, 6.

NUMBER BUILDER

Concepts & Skills

- Understand the processes of addition and subtraction
- Use the language of addition and subtraction
- Discuss part and whole relationships for 10
- See patterns in addition and subtraction
- Use symbolic notation to record addition and subtraction
- Match quantities and numerals
- Share number stories

Ongoing Assessment

1. How can we break 10 apart to make a double?
2. What do we add to 7 to get to 10?
3. Can you tell me a take away story that matches our counters?

Author Notes

"This month the Number Builder displays the quantity of 10 for the children to see and talk about. As in September, the focus of Number Builder for the first two weeks of this month is to help children explore addition, take away, and comparison story problems as they relate to the various arrangements of 10 appearing in the two pockets.

For some variety, you might ask the children to generate every addition and subtraction number sentence that they can think of to match the counters, creating fact families for 10. Around the third week of March a version of *Make the Sum* appears where the parts of 10 are further explored. Finally, during the last week of March, Number Builder becomes a memory game."

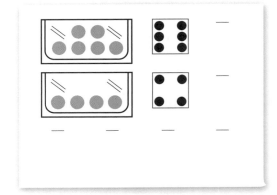

Daily Routine

- Two or three days a week invite volunteers to distribute the 10 counters between the two pockets and clip the corresponding Domino Halves to the right side of the mat.
- Invite children to tell addition or subtraction stories that relate to the display of counters.
- Record one or more stories with words and with a number sentence.
- When all the combinations for 10 have been explored, finish the month playing *Make the Sum* or *Make a Match*.

Ten dogs were
at the park
and 4 ran away.

$$10 - 4 = 6$$

DISCUSSION

For During the Month

Addition and Subtraction Concepts As this month's quantity of 10 is larger than any previous month you may find it necessary to spend more time with extended discussions in order to explore all the possible combinations. Here are some questions you might ask the children to promote their understanding of addition and subtraction concepts.

- Who has a comparing story to share with us?
- What do we need to add to 6 to get to 10?
- How many different ways can we make 10? Let's make a list.

- How many different "take away" number sentences can we write to match our counters?
- How can you figure out the answer to 10 − 1 in your head? 10 − 5?

For Later in the Month

See February, page 90, for a discussion of the various options for Number Builder later in the month.

Number & Operations	Algebra	Geometry	Measurement	Data & Probability
Problem Solving	Reasoning	Communication	Connections	Representation

MEASUREMENT

Concepts & Skills
- Estimate and compare capacity
- Use the language of comparing: *holds the same, holds less,* and *overflows*
- Use nonstandard units to measure capacity

Materials for March

A dishpan of rice placed in a large shallow box; masking tape and marker; a funnel, dustpan, and whisk broom; a collection of unbreakable containers of different shapes and sizes with a minimum capacity of $2\frac{1}{2}$ cups, labeled *A, B, C,* and so on; a measuring scoop

Author Notes

"This month children explore capacity by comparing the capacities of different containers. Everyone has a chance to predict the outcome of pouring one full container into an empty one and talking about the results. At the end of the month, children will have the opportunity to see what equal quantities of rice look like in two different-shaped containers, thus developing their curiosity about capacity."

Daily Routine
- Twice a week for the first weeks of the month show the class one container that you have filled with rice and a second empty container of a different shape.
- Ask the class to predict what will happen when the rice in the full container is poured into the empty one. Will the rice *overflow* the second container, *just fill* it, or *not fill* it?
- Record the number of guesses for each on the board.
- Let a volunteer do the pouring, using a funnel when necessary.
- Have children tell the outcome: Container A holds more than, about the same as, or less than Container B.
- For the last two weeks, demonstrate filling two containers with the same number of scoops and comparing the measured capacity of the two containers.

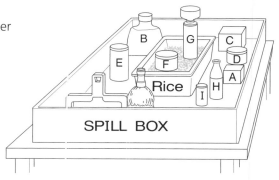

"Do you think the rice from container F will fill container G?"

DISCUSSION

For Throughout the Month

Analyzing Data As time allows, talk about the results of comparing the two containers. You might ask some of the following questions:

- Was anyone surprised by what happened?
- Would someone be willing to share your guess and discuss why you made that guess?
- Did the height or "tallness" of the container matter to you when you made your guess?
- Did you pay more attention to how fat or how wide the container was?
- Did anyone think about both tallness and fatness?
- Were there other things you noticed about the containers that made you guess as you did?
- Do you think it will always be the taller one of the two containers that holds more?
- Do you think a taller container can ever hold less than a shorter container?

Look at the record of the guesses to see if the day's prediction was easy or difficult to make. Did many children make a guess that matched what happened, or did only a few? Have children think about why.

For the End of the Month

Toward the end of the month, try using a nonstandard measurement unit to see how many scoops a container will hold. Choose two containers, one that is tall and skinny and one that is short and fat.

Up the side of the container run a strip of masking tape to mark the level of rice for each scoop emptied into both containers. With the help of the children, fill each container with the same number of scoops.

Estimation, Comparing Here are some questions to pique children's curiosity about volume:

- How many scoops of rice have we collected so far in both containers?
- Look at the two containers that are each holding the same number of scoops. Why do you think the rice comes up higher on one of them?
- Do you think the amount of rice in the two containers is the same or do you think there is more rice in one of them? Why?
- How can we find out if the amount of rice is actually the same?

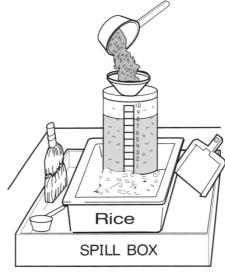

Use scoops to measure and compare the capacity of different containers.

HELPFUL HINTS

- Kitchen funnels do not work well with rice. You can cut off the top third of a plastic 2-liter soft-drink container and invert it to create an efficient funnel.
- Extend the use of nonstandard units by having children tally the number of scoops required to fill the jars. Use the results to make comparisons and order the jars by their capacities.

COUNTING TAPE AND TEN GRIDS

Concepts & Skills

- Develop number sense
- Count with one-to-one correspondence
- Group and count by tens, fives, and ones
- Understand place value
- Compare and order quantities
- Count on and count back
- Use number patterns to add and subtract 10
- Solve problems

Ongoing Assessment

1. How many hundreds, tens, and ones make up today's number?

2. How many groups of ten squares do we see?

3. How many days have we come to school since Day 100? How do you know?

Daily Routine

108 109 110 111 112 113 114 115 116 117 118 119 120

- Repeat the same sequence of colors used for the decades to 100 when putting up squares for Days 101–110, 111–120, 121–130, 131–140, and so on.

- As you record the total number of dots on the Ten Grids, ask children to tell you what digit to write for each place and what it means.

- Refer to both the Counting Tape and the Ten Grids poster to compare patterns in the counting sequence above 100 to patterns in the counting sequence from the beginning of the year.

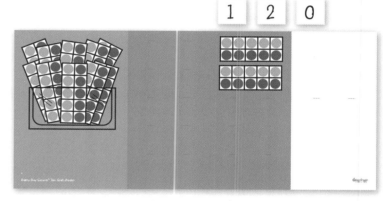

120 is 12 groups of ten.

DISCUSSION

For Throughout the Month

Number Sense, Help children see that the relationships between numbers above 100 are the same as for the numbers up to 100, with a discussion such as the following.

Sample Dialogue

Teacher: What number will we write on today's Counting Tape?

Class: We will write 120.

Teacher: Would someone be willing to share how you decided it would be the 120th day of school?

Child: Yesterday was 119, so today is 120.

Teacher: So you used the counting pattern to figure out that the next number would be 120. Let's say the pattern, beginning with the first day after Day 100.

Class: 101, 102, 103, . . . , 120.

Teacher:	The colors from Day 101 to Day 120 match the colors of 2 groups of ten somewhere else on the Counting Tape. Can you find them?
Child:	The first 2 tens.
Teacher:	Yes, 1 to 20 are the same colors as 101 to 120. Let's count the squares after Day 100 by tens.
Class:	110, 120.
Teacher:	Tell me how to write today's number on today's square.
Class:	One hundred, 2 tens, and 0 ones; 120.
Teacher:	Yes, the 1 is for the first 100, the 2 is for the 2 tens after 100, and the 0 is for no ones. Finally, can you figure out how many groups of ten you have altogether in 120?
Child:	Ten tens to 100 and 2 more; 12 groups of 10.

Continue to include questions that encourage counting on, counting back, adding, and comparing. See September pages 26–27.

Number & Operations	Algebra	Geometry	Measurement	Data & Probability
Problem Solving	Reasoning	Communication	Connections	Representation

COIN COUNTER

Concepts & Skills

- Know the penny, nickel, dime, and quarter
- Know the value of each coin and coin equivalencies
- Count by tens, fives, and ones
- Add mixed coins
- Use mental math, including figuring change
- Record money amounts using both the dollar sign with decimal point and the cent sign
- Solve problems with coins

Materials for March

Coin Cards (TR22) or real coins; 2 rows of 2 small clear pockets; Demo Coins (optional)

Author Notes

"Since it was introduced in November, the Coin Counter has been used to gradually build children's confidence in recognizing and adding combinations of coins. The exchanges between pennies, nickels, dimes, and quarters have made children aware that an amount can be represented with more than one set of coins.

Beginning this month, children will be asked to think up and display in the Counter different combinations of coins whose value equals the day's date. This gives the Coin Counter a problem-solving focus. As children check the total value of the proposed coin combinations placed in the Counter, they gain additional practice counting mixed coins."

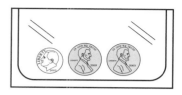

Daily Routine

- Each day ask the class to think of a coin or coins that would add up to the day's date in cents.

- Ask a volunteer to place each combination of coins into its own pocket.

- Have the class check each set of coins placed in the Counter by counting up the total value in unison.

- Finally, record the total for the day in both the dollar sign with decimal point and the cent sign forms below the Counter.

- At the day's end, empty the pockets.

- Once a week hold an extended discussion.

"One dime and two pennies uses the fewest coins for 12 cents."

DISCUSSION

For During the Month

Problem Solving On the first through the fourth of the month, children will be able to suggest only one combination, using pennies. On the fifth through the ninth, they may come up with two ways. From the tenth on, they may think up several combinations of coins. Once a week after the fifth of the month, after children's suggestions of coins for the day are displayed in the Counter, ask them to decide which pocket holds the fewest coins and to think of a way to make the day's date using even fewer coins.

- Which pocket has the fewest coins?

- How many coins are in that pocket?

- Can we make any trades with the coins in that pocket?

- Is it possible to find a solution with fewer coins or is the solution with the fewest coins already displayed?

Addition, Subtraction Now and then ask children to imagine using the coins shown in the Counter to make some small purchases. For example:

- If you take the coins from one row of today's Counter to the store, will you have enough to buy something for 12¢?

- If so, which coins could you give the clerk?

- If not, how much more money would you need?

Occasionally invite children to contribute store problems of their own.

CLOCK

Concepts & Skills

- Experience duration
- Understand analog and digital clocks
- Learn how many minutes are in an hour
- Count by fives and ones
- Read the minute and hour hands

Daily Routine

- The first day, begin with the hands of the Clock showing 9:00 A.M.
- Each day of the month advance the hands of the Clock 5 minutes, having the class count each minute. On the first of March, the hands will stop at 9:05 A.M., on the second, 9:10 A.M., and so forth.
- Draw 5 tally marks each day on a paper near the Clock, giving children another experience counting by fives.
- Finally, record the time in digital form below the Clock and read it together.
- On the 13th of the month, discontinue the use of the Clock or begin another journey around the Clock advancing the hands to 10:05 A.M.

DISCUSSION

For During the Month

Elapsed Time Children often have difficulty with language that describes duration. Frequently asking a question or two similar to those that follow may help children become more familiar with these often confusing terms.

- What time is it right now?
- What time will it be 2 minutes from now?
- In 10 minutes, we'll be going to recess. What time will that be?
- We come in from recess at 10:20. What time will it be 5 minutes after that?
- What time was it 5 minutes ago?
- How many minutes have passed since 9:00?

HELPFUL HINTS

- To encourage children to use their clock-reading skills to interpret the hands on the classroom clock, invite children to raise their hand when they "catch" the classroom clock showing the time that matches the time shown on the bulletin board Clock for the day.
- To let children explore counting by fives, show them how to use the constant feature of their calculators.
  (Press the buttons + 5 = = = ...)

Ongoing Assessment

1. (with Clock showing 10:35) What time does the clock show?
2. Set the Clock to 11:35 for me.
3. How many minutes are between each number on the Clock?

How many minutes past 9:00 does our Clock show?

Number & Operations　　Algebra　　Geometry　　Measurement　　Data & Probability
Problem Solving　　Reasoning　　Communication　　Connections　　Representation

GRAPH

Concepts & Skills

- Collect and record data on a graph
- Read and interpret data on a bar graph
- Count and compare small quantities
- Sample and generalize

Materials for March

Every Day Graph (TR15); several $1\frac{3}{4}$" square paper markers in a bright color; paper sack

Author Notes

"In March, we suggest using the Graph to display the results of a preference poll or class survey. Children enjoy sharing their opinions. The following are examples of questions often posed to children when graphing their interests.

- Which of these pets would you most like to have?
- Would you prefer to eat a chocolate, vanilla, or strawberry ice cream cone?
- Which of these four colors do you like the best?
- Which of these four outdoor activities would you enjoy doing most?
- Which of these three school activities do you enjoy the most?
- Which of these three stories did you enjoy the most?

It is this last suggestion of a Favorite Book Graph that we have chosen to use as an example of a preference poll for March. But any question you or the children choose will produce data and a graph your class will be interested in analyzing. Let the class know there are no right or wrong answers to a preference poll. If more people prefer strawberry ice cream, it doesn't make it the right choice for you if chocolate is your favorite. Having different ideas and opinions makes the class interesting. Sometimes children who made a choice not shared by many of their classmates appreciate some reassurance, even when there are no names on the markers."

Daily Routine

- Create a Graph over the period of one week. Discuss several times during that week and later in the month.
- At the start of the week conduct the survey. (See Discussion.)
- Have each child prepare a colored marker that indicates his or her preference.
- Put all the markers into a sack.
- For several days, have volunteers pull four or five markers at random out of the class's collection and attach them to the Graph.

Ongoing Assessment

1. How many people's opinions are shown on our Graph?
2. Do we have enough markers up yet to predict which choice will have the most when the whole class sample is graphed?
3. What do we know about our class by looking at this Graph?

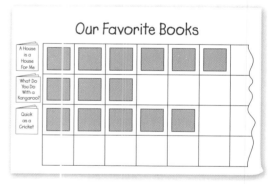

Our Favorite Books

"Do we have enough markers up yet to know which book most people chose?"

DISCUSSION

For the Beginning of Each Week

Collecting Data Pose a survey question (chosen by you or the class) to the children. Ask them to copy down their choice from the possible answers (without consulting others) onto their own graphing marker. They do not need to put their names on the markers. Anonymity tends to make children respond more freely without worrying about what others will think of their choice. Don't forget to include yourself.

Creating a Graph Involve the class in constructing the Graph, deciding how to cut and tape copies of the Graph paper (TR15) to create a grid suited to the data collected.

- How many rows do we need for the categories?
- Can we predict how many spaces we'll need for the longest row?
- What is the most we could need?
- Is it likely that we'll need that many?

Let a few children share their thinking.

For Later in Each Week

Analyzing Data Each time a volunteer draws 5 or 6 more markers to attach to the Graph, a more complete picture of the entire class's preferences becomes apparent. Each day that you add data, get children thinking with questions such as the following.

- Does the new data change your thinking about what the entire Graph will look like when everyone's marker is up?
- Does the choice that had the most markers yesterday still have the most or does a different choice have more now?
- Do we have enough markers up yet to predict which choice will have the most when the whole class sample is graphed?

For When All the Markers Have Been Graphed

Analyzing Data When the Graph finally represents everyone's choices, focus the class on interpreting the data. After reminding children that the less popular choices were just as right for those who made them as the most popular choice, ask some questions that help them analyze the final results.

- What does our Graph tell us?
- What do we know about our class's choices from the Graph?
- Was one choice made by a lot more people or did the choice with the most only have a few more people who chose it?
- How many people's opinions are shown on our Graph?
- How many markers are on our Graph in all?
- Could someone share how you got your total?
- Did we think our Graph would turn out like this when it only had ten markers?
- Were ten markers enough for us to make a good prediction?

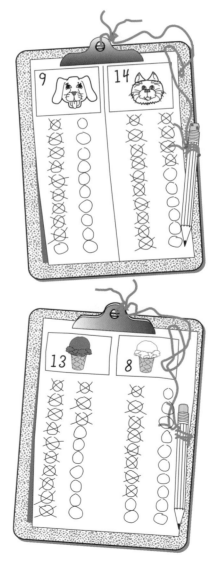

Children enjoy doing surveys of their own.

HELPFUL HINTS

- When asking questions about a graph, it is helpful to provide a "thinking time" for children who need some time to reflect without being influenced by the quick responders. During these few seconds of "thinking time," no one is allowed to call out answers. After this quiet time, some teachers say, "Class," as a signal that anyone who wants to answer can join in for a group response. This is an easy way to become aware of the level of confidence in the class and the proportion of correct and incorrect answers. Some children who are not inclined to raise their hands and offer their thinking when everyone's attention is on them are more likely to respond as part of a group. For questions with correct answers, the focus can switch from the answers to the strategies different class members use to get their answers. Asking frequently, "Would someone be willing to share how they got __ for an answer?" helps everyone see different ways of approaching the question. Building this kind of sharing into class discussions helps children see strategies they might not have used and helps them become better communicators.

- Children often enjoy doing surveys of their own. Allow children to decide on their own survey questions and to carry clipboards around, polling their classmates during a "choosing time" work period. Limiting the class to two pollsters on any one day keeps interruptions of the other children's pursuits to a minimum. Most classmates enjoy being asked to give their opinion or preference and having someone care enough to mark it down. The different polls form a display of considerable interest to the group—so many comparisons to make and so much to talk about!

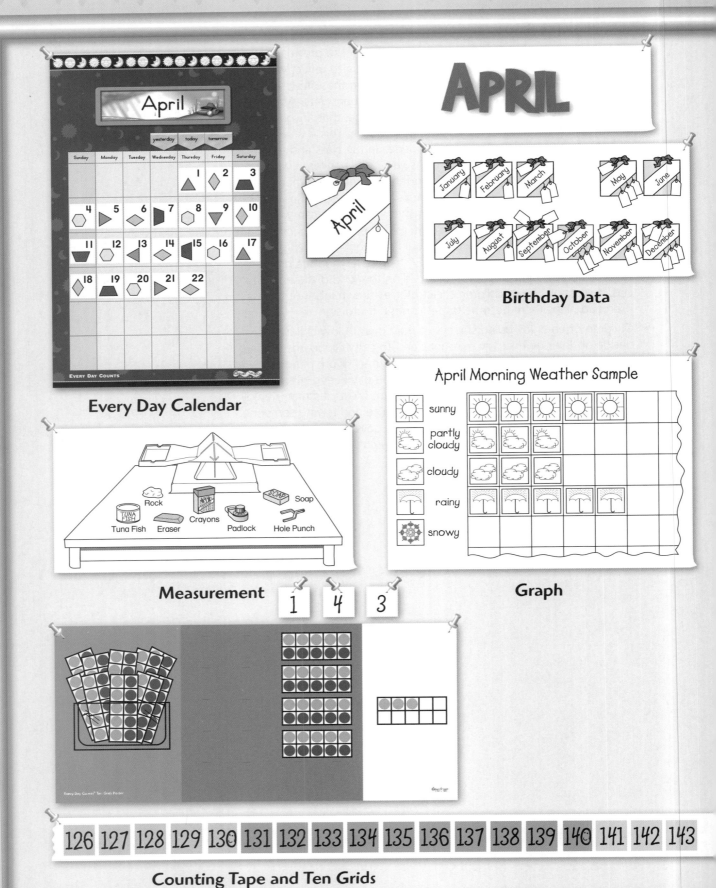

APRIL

Birthday Data

Every Day Calendar

Measurement

Graph

Counting Tape and Ten Grids

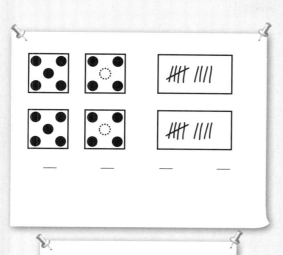

$$5 + 5 = 10$$
$$4 + 4 = 8$$
$$10 \text{ and } 8 \text{ is } 18.$$

Number Builder

Today we have
$ __0.22__ or __22__ ¢.

Coin Counter

APRIL ELEMENTS

In April, the Counting Tape and Ten Grids continue with their progression of three-digit numbers while Number Builder explores combinations for quantities 11 through 18. With the April Coin Counter children are challenged to find several coin combinations to make a total equal to the day's date. Measurement this month invites children to estimate how the weights of various classroom objects compare and then use a balance scale to check their predictions. The Graph keeps track of the spring weather, providing a sample to compare with fall and winter data.

CALENDAR

Concepts & Skills

- Recognize, analyze, and predict patterns
- Know the days of the week and months of the year in order
- Count with one-to-one correspondence to 30
- Read, compare, and order numbers to 30
- Count on and count back
- Match quantities with numerals
- Explore the pattern block shapes as they rotate
- Solve problems using mental math
- Interpret organized data

Ongoing Assessment

1. What is the same about all of the blue and red shapes?
2. What shape do you think will appear in one week?
3. What shape will be displayed on the last day of this month?

Author Notes

"This month's pattern will provide opportunities for much discussion. Even though only 4 different shapes are used in this pattern, their rotation with each repetition will allow for additional investigation. Is a rhombus a rhombus no matter which way it points? What about a trapezoid or a triangle? What happens to the hexagon when it is turned? Are these shapes still the same shape and the same size when turned? With exploration, answers to these questions will most likely surface over the course of the month."

Daily Routine

- Add a Calendar Piece each day.
- After 8 days or more encourage children to predict the position of the next piece as well as its shape and color.

DISCUSSION

For the Beginning of the Month

Problem Solving Ask questions that involve children in adding and comparing the sets of tags on the different packages. For example:

- I see a month that has 4 more birthdays than January has. Which month could this be?
- I see 2 months that have 7 birthdays in all. One month has 1 fewer birthday than the other month. What are the two months?

When there is more than one possible solution, ask children to search for other possibilities.

For the End of the Second Week

Algebraic Thinking In addition to asking children to predict the next day's piece, we can ask them to determine the color, the shape, and possibly the position of the piece that will appear in one week, two weeks, or on the last day of the month. This encourages a variety of counting on and mental math strategies.

The April Calendar Pieces use green triangles, blue rhombuses, red trapezoids, and yellow hexagons to create an ABCD pattern. Each shape rotates 90 degrees with each repetition.

Some children will count all the spaces to the designated space. Others will count full weeks as seven and will use the columns on the Calendar to quickly locate the space. Invite children to share how they came up with their predictions of the shape and color so the group can see several approaches.

Ask children to make predictions two or three more times during the month to give them a chance to use their strategies again or to try out someone else's strategy the next time.

At another time, continue to have manipulatives available so that children can create a version of the month's ABCD pattern on their own.

For the End of the Month

Patterns On one of the last days of April, ask children to look for some patterns to point out to the class. The color pattern will make several diagonals stand out. The multiples of 4 will all be the same color, providing exposure once again to a variety of patterns. You might want to record children's comments and any number patterns they point out on a large piece of paper.

April Pattern

This pattern goes green, blue, red, yellow and repeats.

The pattern always stays the same even though the shapes turn.

If we look at the sides, it goes three sides, four sides, four sides, six sides over and over.

They all go down like stairs.

Number & Operations	Algebra	Geometry	Measurement	Data & Probability
Problem Solving	Reasoning	Communication	Connections	Representation

NUMBER BUILDER

Concepts & Skills

- Understand the processes of addition and subtraction
- Use the language of addition and subtraction (take away and comparison)
- Discuss part and whole relationships for sums 11 through 18
- See patterns in addition and subtraction
- Use symbolic notation to record addition and subtraction
- Match quantities and numerals
- Share number stories

Materials for April

4 Dotted Domino Halves for 5 (TR7); two 3" × 5" index cards

Ongoing Assessment

1. Convince us that this is 15.
2. What do you add to 5 to get to 8? 7? 9?
3. What is the sum of 8 + 8? How did you figure this out?

Author Notes

"Instead of focusing on one quantity for the entire month, April's Number Builder looks at sums 11 through 18, and includes a review of doubles and doubles plus one. Children will explore a variety of ways to use smaller, friendlier quantities to compose and decompose the larger quantities by coloring dots on Dotted Domino Halves instead of using counters. Tally marks will provide an additional visual representation."

Daily Routine

- Use Dotted Domino Halves in place of counters in plastic pockets on the Number Builder Mat.
- On day 1, color one dot on the top Dotted Domino and make 1 tally mark on the top tally card. Continue coloring a dot and making a tally mark each day through day 5.
- On day 6 color a dot on a new Dotted Domino below. Add a tally mark to a new tally card below.
- For days 11–18, alternately color dots on two new blank Dominoes to the right of the full Dominoes. (On day 11, Dominoes for 5 and 1 are in the top row, and a 5 by itself is on the bottom row. On day 12, Dominoes for 5 and 1 are still in the top row and Dominoes for 5 and 1 are in the bottom row.
- Every day have the class tell what they see. Discuss the total amount showing and how you could count it.
- Have children offer addition, subtraction and comparison stories to go with the colored Domino dots and the tally marks.
- Invite the children to record the number sentences that correspond to the stories.

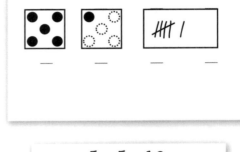

$$5 + 5 = 10$$
$$2 + 1 = 3$$
$$10, 11, 12, 13$$

Use Dotted Dominoes and tally marks to show the day's total.

DISCUSSION

For the Beginning of the Month

For the first ten days the children will have opportunities to focus on adding quantities to 5. They will see 5 + 1, 5 + 2, 5 + 3, 5 + 4, and 5 + 5 as the bottom Domino and the tally grow over these five days. Many children comfortably group and chunk around fives and this will give them time to decompose numbers into 5+ facts.

For After the Tenth Day

On the 13th day a discussion similar to the following might occur in your classroom.

Sample Dialogue

Teacher: Yesterday, our Number Builder had 6 and 6. If we color one more dot on the top Domino, we know that we will have 13, but how could we check this?

Child: We could start by adding the 2 fives to make 10. That leaves us with a 2 and a 1, and that makes 3. We could count 10, 11, 12, 13. We have 13.

Teacher: Where did these 2 fives come from?

Child: One of the fives came from the 5 and 2 for 7 and one of the fives came from the 5 and 1 for 6.

Teacher: You broke the 7 apart to get 5 and 2, and you broke the 6 apart to get 5 and 1. That's nice. How could we show what we have done with numbers?

Child: We could write 5 + 5 = 10 and 1 + 2 = 3.

Teacher: Would we be done yet?

Child: No, we need to add the 3 and the 10. That's hard.

Child: Oh, that's 13.

Teacher: 10 + 3 = 13. What a good job of breaking these numbers apart and making them work for you. You broke 6 and 7 apart in a friendly way to get to 13.

Continue to look at each day's quantity through the eyes of your children. Validate all the various strategies that they use to add these larger quantities.

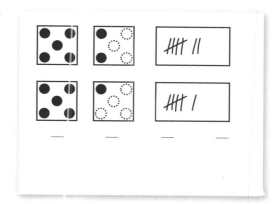

Mom made 13 snacks and we ate 6. How many are left?

Helpful Hints

- After the 18th of the month take the opportunity to review Domino Cards that you have previously made for combinations of 5 through 10. These cards may be arranged by sums, but also allow for many other sorting options as you have experienced in previous months.

- You might again consider sorting out the +0, +1, or +2 cards for a quick workout. The doubles could also be sorted and practiced.

- As previously mentioned, some teachers like to play *Quick As You Can* holding up the Domino Cards and asking the children to respond with a sum as quickly as they can.

Number & Operations	Algebra	Geometry	Measurement	Data & Probability
Problem Solving	Reasoning	Communication	Connections	Representation

Measurement

Concepts & Skills
- Estimate and compare weights
- Learn the language of comparing weight: *heavy*, *light*, *heavier*, and *lighter*

Materials for April

A balance scale; a collection of common objects in different shapes, sizes, and weights (a can of tuna or soup, box of crayons, hole punch, chalkboard eraser, and so on), labeled *A, B, C,* etc.; masking tape; two 17" × 11" record sheets

Author Notes

"This month's activities foster children's understanding of the concept of weight and comparing weight. Everyone will have an opportunity to predict which of two objects weighs more and then watch the comparisons be made."

Ongoing Assessment

1. (offering two objects different in weight) Which is heavier?

2. (putting two objects on the balance scale) Which is heavier? Which is lighter?

3. (offering two objects equal in weight) Which is heavier or are they about the same weight?

Daily Routine

- Show the class two objects varying in size and weight. Have the children heft the two objects to determine which is heavier.
- Have children estimate which of the objects is heavier without hefting. Record guesses for each object.
- Encourage children to use words such as *heavier* and *lighter*, or *weighs more*, *weighs less*, or *weighs the same* to describe the result of comparing the objects.
- Let a volunteer put them on the scale so the children can check their predictions.
- State the resulting comparison: "The book is heavier than the scissors, and the scissors are lighter than the book."

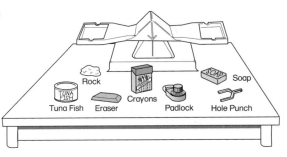

"Which object do you think might be heaviest?"

DISCUSSION

For Early in the Month

As you introduce children to this month's measurement activity you might have a conversation similar to the following.

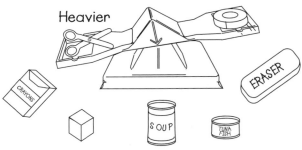

"Did you guess that the scissors was heavier than the tape?"

Sample Dialogue

Teacher: This is a balance scale.

Teacher: Let's predict which is heavier, these crayons or these markers. Remember that heavier means it will feel like you are holding more.

Child: The crayons.

Child: I think the markers.

Teacher: I will ask Siryah to help do the weighing with me. Raise your hand if you think the crayons are heavier? Okay, seven people raised their hand. Now raise your hand if you think the markers are heavier. Siryah, put the markers on one end of the scale and put the crayons on the other. What happened, class?

Child: The scale showed the crayons are heavier than the markers.

Teacher: Good. The crayons are heavier than the markers and the markers are lighter than the crayons.

For Throughout the Month

Estimation For the rest of the month, continue to have children guess which object weighs more and let them use the balance scale to check their guesses. Pose the following questions to develop the language of comparing weight:

- Which is heavier, the _____ or the _____?
- Which is lighter, the _____ or the _____?
- Did you think about the size of the object when you made your guess?
- Will the larger of two objects always be the heavier?
- Did anyone think about having held similar objects before and how heavy they felt in your hands?
- Did anyone use past days' comparisons to help make a guess today?

HELPFUL HINTS

- Some children may want to compare three objects and order them. Then the objects would be classified as *light, lighter, lightest* or *heavy, heavier, heaviest.*

- To help preserve the scale, limit the number of children to two at a time, making sure that everyone has a turn. If you have access to another scale you might want to get it so more children can experiment with comparing.

Number & Operations	Algebra	Geometry	Measurement	Data & Probability
Problem Solving	Reasoning	Communication	Connections	Representation

COUNTING TAPE AND TEN GRIDS

Concepts & Skills

- Develop number sense
- Count with one-to-one correspondence
- Group and count by tens, fives, and ones
- Understand place value
- Compare and order quantities
- Count on and count back
- Use number patterns to add and subtract 10
- Solve problems

Daily Routine

- Repeat the same sequence of colors used for the decades to 100 when putting up squares for Days 101–110, 111–120, 121–130, 131–140, and so on.

131 132 133 134 135 136 137 138 139 140 141 142 143

- As you record the total number of dots on the Ten Grids, ask children to tell you what digit to write for each place and what it means.

1 4 3

- Refer to both the Counting Tape and the Ten Grids poster to compare patterns in the counting sequence above 100 to patterns in the counting sequence from the beginning of the year.

DISCUSSION

For During the Month

Place Value Continue to use the Ten Grids to prompt discussions focused on place value. Frequently ask the class to suggest different ways to count to check the total. To encourage children to think in hundreds, tens, and ones, occasionally ask them, "How much would we have if we added (or subtracted) a hundred? A ten? A single dot?"

Number Sense Continue to focus on ways that the counting pattern for numbers above 100 is like the sequence up to 100. For example,

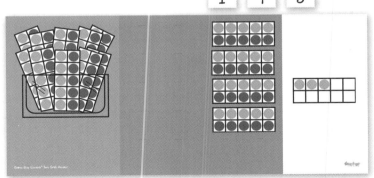

"How much would we have if we took away a hundred?"

© Great Source. Copying is prohibited.

Day 143 follows Day 142 just as Day 43 followed Day 42. See March, page 108 for discussion suggestions. To foster number sense, continue to include questions that encourage counting on, counting back, comparing, and adding and subtracting.

HELPFUL HINTS

- If you need display space for the new Daily Domino and Measuring activities in April, consider retiring the Ten Grids for the rest of the year. Its main goal, exposing children to three-place numbers and the counting pattern above 100, has been met.

- If Day 150 arrives in April, take the time to talk about 50 being one half of 100. (See November's Day 50 Discussion on page 56.) Encourage children to estimate where Day 200 might come on the Counting Tape if school were to last until then.

Number & Operations   Algebra   Geometry   Measurement   Data & Probability
Problem Solving   Reasoning   Communication   Connections   Representation

COIN COUNTER

Concepts & Skills

- Know the penny, nickel, dime, and quarter
- Know the value of each coin and coin equivalencies
- Count by tens, fives, and ones
- Determine the value of a collection of coins
- Use mental math, including figuring change
- Record money amounts using both the dollar sign with decimal point and the cent sign
- Solve problems with coins

Daily Routine

- As in March, each day ask the class to think of a coin or coins that would add up to the day's date in cents.
- Ask a volunteer to place each combination of coins into its own pocket.
- Have the class check each set of coins placed in the Counter by counting up the total value in unison.
- Finally, record the total for the day in both the dollar sign with decimal point and the cent sign forms below the Counter.
- At the day's end, empty the pockets.
- Once a week hold an extended discussion.

Ongoing Assessment

1. If I have 16 cents, what coins could I have?

2. If you have 2 dimes and buy a pencil for 16 cents, what change should you get back?

3. How can we make 28 cents using the fewest coins?

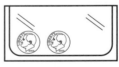

"Are there any other ways to make 20 cents?"

DISCUSSION

For During the Month

Problem Solving Once a week, after children's suggestions of coins for the day are displayed in the Coin Counter, ask them to consider the display.

- Which pocket holds the fewest coins?
- Can you think of a way to make the day's date using even fewer coins?
- Is it possible to use fewer coins, or is the solution with the fewest coins already displayed in the Coin Counter?

Mental Math Occasionally, ask children to imagine using the coins shown in the Counter to make some small purchases. Children may enjoy suggesting store problems of their own.

- If you were to take the coins from one row of today's Coin Counter to the store, would you have enough to buy something for 15¢?
- If so, which coins would you give the clerk?
- If not, how much more money would you need?

"What coins should we use to pay for this?"

HELPFUL HINTS

- Gather a "play store" collection of a few objects labeled with prices to 40¢. A volunteer draws one item out of the store box and the class decides (depending on its price) which coins to use to purchase it.
- This is an opportunity for children to use calculators. If children make purchases without the exact amount, they can use a calculator to check whether they got the correct change.

Number & Operations	Algebra	Geometry	Measurement	Data & Probability
Problem Solving	Reasoning	Communication	Connections	Representation

GRAPH

Concepts & Skills

- Collect and record data on a graph over time
- Read and interpret data on a picture or bar graph
- Count and compare small quantities

Materials for April

Graph (TR15) made to match the ones assembled in October and January for sampling the weather; Weather Markers (TR16); Weather Graphs from October and January

Author Note

"The Every Day Graph provides a record of a weather sample in October, January, and April. Graphing the weather again this month allows the class the opportunity to compare the kinds of weather that occurred in your area in the fall and winter with the kinds of weather that appear in the spring."

Ongoing Assessment

1. Does our sample show more cloudy days or sunny days? How many more?
2. How many school days would it need to rain for the rainy days to equal the cloudy days?
3. Which were the best months for riding a bike?

Daily Routine

- Once again have the class look outside at the same time each day and decide what the weather is like at that moment.
- Have a volunteer attach the appropriate Weather Marker to the Graph.
- Update daily and discuss once a week.

DISCUSSION

For the First Day

Creating a Graph Instead of preparing the Weather Graph ahead of time, involve children in setting it up. Tell children you want to create a Graph that has the same headings in the same order as the October and January Weather Graphs so that it will be easy to compare the information gathered during the three different seasons. With the old graphs in view, ask questions such as these:

- How should we label our April Weather Graph?
- Do you think the same length will work out or do you think it will need to be longer or shorter? Why?

Predicting Looking at the October and January Graphs, ask the class to consider the following types of questions.

- Who thinks there will be more sunny days in the April sample than in the fall and winter samples?
- How about rainy days—more, fewer, or the same?
- How about snowy days?

It will be interesting to see how the three weather samples compare by month's end.

For During the Month

Analyzing Data Occasionally ask the types of comparing questions that might lead children to analyze the data.

- What kind of weather have we had most often?
- How many sunny days have we graphed so far this month?
- Is there any kind of weather we haven't seen on school days yet?
- Does our sample show more cloudy days or sunny days? How many more?
- How many school days would it need to rain for the rainy days to equal the cloudy days?
- How many days' weather are shown on the Graph?
- Does our Graph show all days in April to this day?

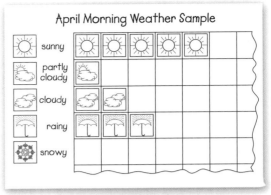

"How many days have we graphed altogether?"

For the End of the Month

Focus student attention on the three graphs showing fall, winter, and spring weather samples. Before making any comparisons, count up the total days represented on each graph to make sure the samples are close enough in size to allow fair comparisons. (Each graph should have 17 to 20 Weather Markers.) You might start with an open-ended question such as, "What do we know about our fall, winter, and spring weather from the samples shown on these graphs? What do these graphs tell us?" After children have offered many observations and comparisons of their own, you might follow up with a few questions:

- Which month had the most sunny days?
- Which month had nearly the same number of partly cloudy and sunny days?
- Which month had the most rainy days? The fewest?
- Which months had the same total of cloudy and rainy days together?
- Which were the best months for riding a bike?
- Which month had the most of your favorite weather?

HELPFUL HINTS

- If your school year includes a vacation break in April, you'll need to keep a record of the weather during vacation. Otherwise, the April sample at month's end will be too small to compare to the October and January data.
- As suggested in January, you may want to use the newspaper to graph the weather of a city in another part of the country to compare to your own spring weather. (See January, page 83.)

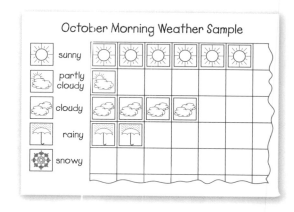

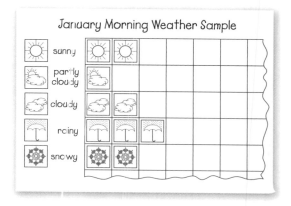

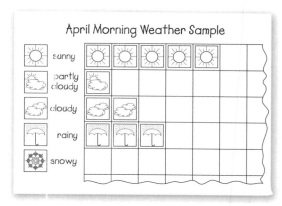

"Which month had most of your favorite weather?"

MAY

Every Day Calendar

Birthday Data

What shape did you bring in?

cylinders	Kate	Alec	Riam	Juan		
spheres	Sarah	Kate	Mr. G.			
rectangular boxes	Matt	Elise	Manuel	Maria	Yoshi	Tiffany
cubes	Jenny					
other						

Graph

1 6 5

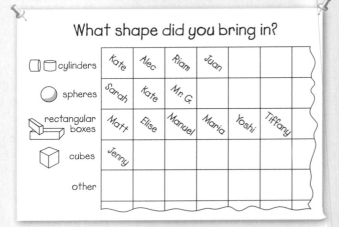

| 148 | 149 | 150 | 151 | 152 | 153 | 154 | 155 | 156 | 157 | 158 | 159 | 160 | 161 | 162 | 163 | 164 | 165 |

Counting Tape and Ten Grids

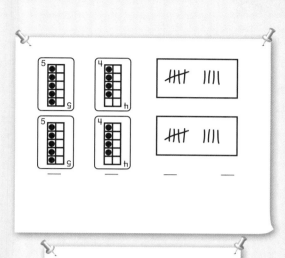

I have 9 cents
and Sarah has
9 cents. How much
more does Sarah have?
9 – 9 = 0

Number Builder

24¢

24¢ + 1¢ = 25¢.

Coin Counter

As the school year winds down, so does Every Day Counts Calendar Math. The Calendar provides one more new pattern to analyze. Counting Tape and Ten Grids continues right up to the very last day of school. Number Builder offers another way to look at combinations for up to 18, and Coin Counter provides a new experience in figuring change for purchases. The Graph provides motivation for the class to search for geometric shapes in the environment. Graphing everyone's responses to the question, "Which part of Calendar Math helped me learn the most?" might provide a fitting end-of-the-year activity. While no two groups are alike, children's answers might help you to evaluate your successes and to plan modifications for next year.

Number & Operations   Algebra   Geometry   Measurement   Data & Probability
Problem Solving   Reasoning   Communication   Connections   Representation

CALENDAR

Concepts & Skills

- Recognize, analyze, and predict patterns
- Know the days of the week and months of the year in order
- Count with one-to-one correspondence to 31
- Read, compare, and order numbers to 31
- Count on and count back
- Match quantities with numerals
- Solve problems using mental math
- Interpret organized data
- Explore and describe the attributes of three-dimensional shapes

Daily Routine

- Add a Calendar Piece each day.
- Use the May Birthday Packages as a focus for problem solving.
- As the pattern emerges, encourage children to predict the position of each block in the stack for the next day's Calendar Piece.

DISCUSSION

For the Beginning of the Month

Have the class name the months in order, beginning with January. Go through the sequence again, stopping with a clap on the present month. Note that May is the fifth month of the year.

Feature May's Package near the Calendar and have children help place the tags. Engage children by posing questions such as the following.

- How many birthdays do we have in May?
- Who has the first birthday in May?
- Where does this tag belong?
- Who has the second birthday?
- How many days do we have to wait between these two birthdays? How did you figure that out?

DISCUSSION

For the End of the Second Week of May

Algebraic Thinking, Mental Math Discuss the new pattern that appears on the May Calendar. In addition to asking children to predict the next day's piece, extend their thinking with questions such as the following.

- What will the stack of blocks look like next Monday?
- Which block will be on top one week from today?
- Which block will be on top two weeks from today?
- When will the red cylinder next be on the top of the stack?

The May/June Calendar Pieces use stacked cubes, rectangular prisms, and cylinders to display a simple ABC pattern, but there are options for many interpretations.

These prediction questions encourage a variety of counting on and mental math strategies. Invite children to share how they came up with their predictions.

Three-Dimensional Shapes You may want to collect some blocks, including a `cube` , a `rectangular solid` , and a cylinder to stack. Review the attributes of these shapes, looking at surfaces or faces, corners, and edges. Generating ways to describe the various stacks will help when predicting future arrangements. They might be described as can on top, box on top, and cube on top. Someone else might see surfaces as curved, flat, flat when looking at the top shape. Another interpretation might include looking at faces of the top shape and stating circle, rectangle, square. Others might choose to look at the shape in the middle or on the bottom for a pattern.

To Sum Up

On one of the last days of May, ask children to share all of the patterns that they see on the Calendar. You might want to play *Name the Hidden Piece*. Remove 4 or 5 pieces from the Calendar and hold just one of them in your hand as the hidden piece. Invite the children to guess the hidden piece by using only "math talk." These are some of the questions to encourage children to ask:

- Does it have a curved shape on top?
- Does the top block have all faces that are the same?
- Does the bottom block have rectangles on it?
- Is there a square block in the middle?
- Is the number on it a neighbor of 10?
- Does it have two numbers on it?
- Does it come between 8 and 10?

For the Beginning of June

If your school year extends into June, mention that June signals an end to spring and the beginning of summer. You might also point out that as the sixth month of the year, when June is over the year is half over.

Problem Solving Attach the June month strip, and reuse the May/June Calendar Pieces to elicit further observations. Each day, as a new stack goes up, ask children to predict the number and description of the stack that will come up in one week, two weeks, and three weeks.

- June 19 is the last day of school. What will the stack look like on June 19? How did you figure that out?
- What do you think June 20 will look like? Why do you think so?
- June 3, June 6, and June 9 all have the yellow cube on top. What other days do you think will have a yellow cube on top?
- What are three days that show a blue box at the top of the stack? What will be the next day that has a blue box at the top?

After entertaining suggestions, place the blocks for these future days on the Calendar. Allow time for children to explain how they were able to predict the number and the shape of the stack.

This pattern also allows for investigating of groups of three. Since a new group of three blocks is added each day, there will be options to count by threes, write number sentences adding 3 each day, and predict the total number of blocks after one day, two days, three days, and so on.

"Is it between 8 and 10?"

"Is it a neighbor of 10?"

"Does it have a square block on top?"

"Does it have 2 numbers on it?"

"Does it have rectangles as sides on the top block?"

"What will the stack look like on June 19?"

HELPFUL HINT

- Since the pattern for threes is highlighted on the Calendar this month, involve children in brainstorming a list of things that come in threes. Then, using the list, everyone can suggest story problems that involve counting by threes. For example, 3 tricycles would need how many wheels?

Number & Operations	Algebra	Geometry	Measurement	Data & Probability
Problem Solving	Reasoning	Communication	Connections	Representation

NUMBER BUILDER

Concepts & Skills

- Understand the processes of addition and subtraction
- Use the language of addition and subtraction
- Discuss part and whole relationships for sums 11 through 18
- See patterns in addition and subtraction
- Use symbolic notation to record addition and subtraction
- Match quantities and numerals
- Share number stories

Materials for May

Four sets of 1–5 Ten Grid Cards (TR8); two 3" × 5" index cards

Author Notes

"The May Number Builder will again display a quantity that increases by one each day displaying totals of 6–18. In place of counters or Dotted Domino Cards, 1–5 Ten Grid Cards will be used to revisit doubles and doubles + 1 as well as the "pulling out the fives" addition strategies. Continue to look at each day's quantity through the eyes of your children. Validate the various strategies that they use to add these larger quantities."

Daily Routine

- **On day 1** clip the Ten Grid card for 1 to the left side of the Number Builder mat. Draw 1 tally mark on a new index card clipped to the right side of the mat. Then, each day through day 5, replace the Ten Grid card with the one for 1 more, and add 1 tally mark to the index card.
- **On day 6** clip a second Ten Grid card, showing 1, below the first, and draw 1 tally mark on a second index card clipped below the first.
- **On days 7–10** replace the bottom Ten Grid card with the cards for 2, then 3, 4, and 5 to create 5 + 2, 5 + 3, 5 + 4, and 5 + 5. Add 1 tally mark each day as well.
- **Then, on days 11–19,** alternately clip Ten Grid cards showing one more dot to the right of one of the two cards showing 5. For instance, on the 12th day, the Ten Grid cards for 5 and 1 are shown on the top as well as on the bottom to show 6 + 6. Continue to show doubles and neighbors until you have reached 9 + 9.

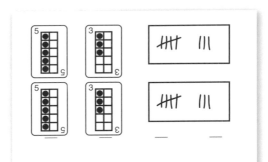

I have 8 cents and Sarah has 8 cents. How much more does Sarah have?
8 - 8 = 0

- For each new display, let children offer addition, take-away subtraction and comparison subtraction stories to go with the Ten Grid Cards displayed.
- Have the class tell what they see and invite the children to record the number sentences that correspond to the stories.

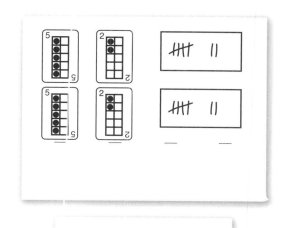

DISCUSSION

For Throughout the Month

Additional Strategies You might want to use some of the following questions to foster understanding of adding quantities to five and decomposing numbers.

- What do I add to 5 to get to 6? 7? 8? 9?
- Convince us that this is 17.
- How might you break 9 apart to help you look at 9 + 9?
- Does anyone have another way you like to look at 9 + 9?
- Did we make a double today? How do you know?
- What will tomorrow's neighbors problem be?
- Why do we call that a doubles plus one?
- What do you think the next day's doubles will be?

$$7 + 6 = 13$$
$$6 + 7 = 13$$
$$13 - 6 = 7$$
$$13 - 7 = 6$$

"What was yesterday's double? What will tomorrow's double be?"

HELPFUL HINT

- If you have extra days at the end of the month, take the opportunity to review combinations of 5 through 10 with the Domino Cards that you have made in previous months. Take time to focus on the cards adding onto five (5 + 1, 5 + 2, 5 + 3, 5 + 4 and 5 + 5).

Number & Operations	Algebra	Geometry	Measurement	Data & Probability
Problem Solving	Reasoning	Communication	Connections	Representation

COUNTING TAPE AND TEN GRIDS

Concepts & Skills

- Develop number sense
- Count with one-to-one correspondence
- Group and count by tens, fives, and ones
- Understand place value
- Compare and order quantities
- Count on and count back
- Use number patterns to add and subtract 10 or 100
- Use the language of duration
- Use mental math

Ongoing Assessment

1. How many groups of ten squares do we see? How many extra ones?
2. How many school days have we had since Day 100?
3. How many school days have we had since Day 150?

Daily Routine

- Frequently look back at the whole Tape during discussions.
- Engage children in year-end wrap-up activities described in Helpful Hints.
- Tell children how many days are in the school year, and focus some question on how many days of school are left.

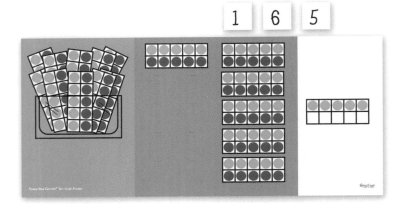

"How many days of school have we had since day 150?"

DISCUSSION

During the Month

Number Sense As the last day of school approaches, tell children the number of the last day of school so they can determine the days left in the school year. Encourage children to share the variety of mental math strategies they use to compute this difference. Continue to focus on interpreting three-digit numbers and looking for ways the counting pattern above 100 is like the sequence up to 100.

HELPFUL HINTS

- On one of the last days of school, focus the activity on taking down the Counting Tape. Cut the Tape in 10-number intervals, handing out strips (1–10, 11–20, 21–30, and so on) to individual children. Some teachers have the class help construct a giant hundred chart. Children pin up the decade strips of Counting Tape in order, one below the other, ending with 91–100. If holes are punched near the ends of the strips, the strips can be slipped off pins for ordering activities and can then be easily returned to the display. The giant hundred chart provides a focus for pattern searches, which help children see the predictability of the counting sequence.

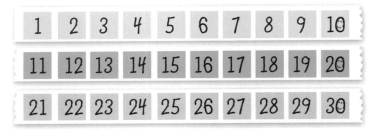

Turn the Counting Tape into a Giant Hundred Chart.

- If you need display space for the large hundred chart, you might consider retiring the Ten Grids poster for the rest of the year. Its main goal has been met.
- Children can color their own Hundred Chart (TR20) to match the large one formed with the cut-apart Counting Tape. The children's copies can accompany them home in June and be used to mark off the days of summer vacation. Children can consider the question, "Do you think we will have marked off 100 days away from school before we come back again at the end of summer?"

COIN COUNTER

Concepts & Skills

- Know the penny, nickel, dime, and quarter
- Know the value of each coin and coin equivalencies
- Count by tens, fives, and ones
- Add mixed coins
- Use mental math, including figuring change
- Record money amounts using both the dollar sign with decimal point and the cent sign
- Solve problems using coins

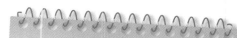

Ongoing Assessment

1. This quarter, nickel, and penny are equal to how many cents in all?

2. If you use a quarter to buy an apple that costs 17 cents, what will your change be?

3. If I have 4 coins that make 16 cents, what are my coins?

Author Notes

"This month the focus is figuring change when a purchase is made with a quarter, now that children have had sufficient practice creating combinations of coins equal to the day's date in March and April. Counting change fosters counting up and other mental math strategies."

Daily Routine

- Through May 25, display an amount in the top row of the Coin Counter equal to the day's date in cents.
- Tell children that this is the cost of the day's imaginary purchase.
- Each day children "pay" for the imaginary item with a quarter and then determine the change due by counting on.
- To show making change for a 12 cent purchase from a quarter, place 3 pennies into the second row of the Counter as the class counts up, "13, 14, 15," and then 2 nickels, perhaps, as the class continues, "20, 25 cents."
- Children can suggest other possible combinations of coins that the clerk could use to count out the correct change.

"13, 14, 15, and 5 more is 20 and 5 more is 25."

HELPFUL HINTS

- The play store is a great opportunity for children to use calculators to confirm the amount of their purchases and their change.
- *Guess My Coins* provides some fun problem solving at year's end. When you draw three empty circles to represent three coins on the board and write their total value, the class works to figure out what coins you have in mind. When solving for three coins becomes too easy, progress to using four coins.

GRAPH

Concepts & Skills

- Recognize three-dimensional and two-dimensional geometric shapes in the environment
- Describe attributes of cylinders, spheres, rectangular solids, and cubes
- Identify and name circles, rectangles, and squares

Materials for May

A collection of boxes, containers, and objects that are cylinders, spheres, rectangular solids, or cubes; Graph paper (TR15); class set of graph markers ($1\frac{3}{4}$" paper squares); watercolor pen; four large posters, one for each shape; advertising supplements from a Sunday newspaper; models of geometric solids (optional)

Author Notes

"This month children are introduced to cylinders, spheres, rectangular solids, and cubes. Each child will have the chance to bring one object from home that fits into one of the categories of shapes. The growth of the class collection of shapes will be recorded on a graph. The emphasis throughout the month will be on modeling and eliciting descriptive geometric language used to distinguish one set of shapes from another."

Daily Routine

- As early in the month as possible, send home the Parent Letter. (See Helpful Hints.)
- The first week, introduce and discuss one of the four shapes each day.
- As children bring in objects from home, ask them to show their shapes to the class and have the children classify each as a can-shaped cylinder, a ball-shaped sphere, a box-shaped rectangular solid, a square, box-shaped cube, or "other."
- Finally, have the day's contributors add markers to the Graph to represent each shape brought in that day.
- Ask the class to suggest a few facts revealed by the Graph.

DISCUSSION

For the Beginning of the Month

Classifying, Geometry Explain that this month the class will be searching for four different geometric shapes at school and at home. Introduce one shape each day. Show the class two or three examples of one of the shapes and have children tell how they are alike. Add your observations, if needed, so the critical attributes of each shape will be pointed out.

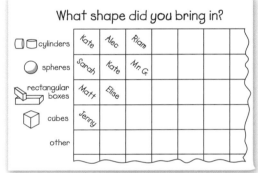

What shape did you bring in?

cylinders	Kate	Alec	Riam			
spheres	Sarah	Kate	Mr. G.			
rectangular boxes	Matt	Elise				
cubes	Jenny					
other						

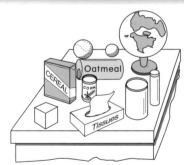

"How many of these shapes are cylinders?"

For cylinders (cans, spice jars, batteries, coins, etc.):
- They're round and they roll.
- The bases or openings on the two ends are matching circles.
- They'll stand on their circle bases.

For spheres (globe, playground ball, orange, marble, etc.):
- They're round and they roll.
- They have no flat faces and will not stack.
- Each has one continuous curved surface.

For rectangular solids (school box, brick, chalkboard eraser, etc.):
- They have six flat faces.
- The faces are in the shape of rectangles (four sides with four square corners).
- They stack easily and do not roll.

For cubes (sugar cube, cubic boxes, wooden cube, etc.):
- They are all rectangular solids.
- Their faces are all special rectangles called squares (four equal sides and four square corners).

Follow this discussion of the attributes with a search for other examples of the three-dimensional shape in the classroom.

When all four shapes have been introduced, label a poster with the name and sketch of each shape. Invite children to cut out pictures of common objects that represent cylinders, spheres, boxes, and cubes from newspaper advertising supplements. Paste these pictures of real-world geometric solids on the appropriate poster.

For Throughout the Month

Have children look for a discarded item at home that can be added to the class collection of cylinders, spheres, rectangular solids, and cubes. The object must be something that doesn't need to be returned. (See the sample letter to parents.) Assemble a Graph and label the rows with the names of the shapes to record the contributions as they come in.

Analyzing Data When children begin to bring in their objects from home, discuss as a group how each shape should be classified. Then discuss the emerging Graph whenever possible. Some questions might include:

- How many items have been brought in so far? How did you get your total or sum?
- What shape do we have the most of now?
- What shape do we have the least of?
- How many more __ than __ do we have?

HELPFUL HINT

- Children enjoy problem solving in the game *Who Am I?* Give children clues, which, when taken together, identify one and only one object in the collection. For example, "I am a rectangular solid, larger than the raisin box, and I used to hold a breakfast food," might narrow the selection to the cereal box.

Dear Parents,

We've been learning to recognize and describe the following geometric shapes in class this month:

— Cylinders (can shapes)

— Spheres (ball shapes)

— Rectangular solids (box shapes)

— Cubes (square box shapes)

Please encourage your child to point out objects in your home that can be classified as cylinders, spheres, rectangular boxes, cubes. The children have been asked to look for a discarded household item headed for the garbage or recycling bin and bring it in to add to the class collection of real-world boxes, cylinders, and spheres.

Thanks for your support with this project. Please do not send anything made of glass.

Sincerely,

BIBLIOGRAPHY

Baratta-Lorton, Mary. "The Opening," *Math Their Way Newsletter* 1977–78. Saratoga, CA: The Center for Innovation in Education.

Baratta-Lorton, Mary. *Mathematics Their Way.* Dale Seymour Publications, 1995.

Baratta-Lorton, Mary. *Workjobs II.* Pearson Learning, 1987.

Burk, Donna, Allyn Snider, and Paula Symonds. "The Calendar," *Box It or Bag It.* Salem, OR: Math Learning Center, 1988.

Burns, Marilyn, and Kathy Richardson. "Making Sense out of Word Problems," *Learning.* January, 1981.

For Good Measure: Principles and Goals for Mathematics Assessment. Washington DC:National Academy Press

Kamii, Constance. *Young Children Reinvent Arithmetic: Implications of Piaget's Theory.* New York: Teachers College Press, 1985.

Kanter, Patsy. *Helping Your Child Learn Math.* U.S. Department of Education, 2000.

Marolda, Maria. *Attribute Games and Activities.* Mountain View, CA: Creative Publications, 1997.

National Council of Teachers of Mathematics. *Assessment in the Mathematics Classroom, The 1993 Yearbook.* Reston, VA: The National Council of Teachers of Mathematics, 1993

National Council of Teachers of Mathematics. *Curriculum and Evaluation Standards for School Mathematics.* Reston, VA: The National Council of Teachers of Mathematics, 1989.

National Council of Teachers of Mathematics. *Mathematics Assessment: Myths, Models, Good Questions and Practical Suggestions.* Reston, VA: The National Council of Teachers of Mathematics, 1991.

Richardson, Kathy. *A Look at Children's Thinking. Video 2 Assessment Techniques: Number Combinations and Place Value.* Norman, OK: Education enrichment, Inc. 1990.

Richardson, Kathy. *Developing Number Concepts Using Unifix Cubes.* Reading, MA: Addison-Wesley, 1984.

Wirtz, Robert. *Banking on Problem Solving* and *Think, Talk, Connect.* Washington, DC: Curriculum Development Assoc., Inc., 1980.

Wirtz, Robert. *Drill and Practice at a Problem-Solving Level.* Washington, DC: Curriculum Development Assoc., Inc., 1976.

Wirtz, Robert. *Making Friends with Numbers, Kit 1: Addition and Subtraction.* Washington, DC: Curriculum Development Assoc., Inc., 1977.

ASSESSMENT INTRODUCTION

To the Teacher:

The Assessment component of **Every Day Counts® Calendar Math** includes four tests: Pretest, Winter Test, Spring Test, and Post Test. This arrangement enables you to monitor student progress at significant times during the year. Each test includes an answer key and an accompanying list of tested skills.

The Pretest and Post Test are parallel tests, measuring skills for the whole year. They include questions in various standardized-test formats, including short answer, multiple choice, and extended response questions.

The Winter and Spring Tests are structured similarly. The Winter Test focuses on skills presented in September, October, and November, and can be given in December or January. The Spring Test covers skills taught in December, January, and February, and can be given in March or April.

Any of these tests will be useful as practice at various times during the year before students take regular standardized tests. They can also be given in shorter form—a page or a few questions at a time—for a quick assessment check.

Following each test is an answer key that includes a list of tested skills, the corresponding test item numbers, and a list of Calendar Math Elements where the skills are presented. This allows you to find places within the program where individual skills can be reinforced in a variety of contexts.

The tests are cumulative in nature, testing skills in ways similar to the way they are taught in Calendar Math, but in slightly different contexts. Students should be able to apply the skills they have learned and experienced in a variety of situations.

Grade 1 teachers:

For each test, give a copy of the test page(s) to children. Write the child's name at the top of each page, or have the child write his or her name. Read the questions aloud and have children mark their answers on the page. You may want to administer these tests to small groups of 3 or 4 children at a time, or to individuals one-on-one. You may also choose to administer only one page of the test each day.

Read each item aloud. (Have children look at the first page.)

1. Look at the pattern of shapes. What should the next two shapes be? Draw the two shapes that come next.

2. Look at the numbers in the boxes. What number comes next? Write the number in the box.

3. Look at the numbers: two, four, six, eight, ten . . . . What numbers come next? Write the next two numbers on the lines.

4. Look at the baseball caps. How many caps are there? Draw a circle around the number that tells how many caps.

5. Look at the blocks. How many blocks are there? Draw a circle around the number that tells how many blocks.

6. Look at the names of the days: Sunday, Tuesday, Wednesday, Saturday. Which day of the week comes just before Monday? Circle the name of the day that comes just before Monday.

7. Look at the names of the months: January, March, October, December. Which month comes next after November? Circle the name of the month that comes next after November.

8. Look at the numbers. Which number has a two in the ones place? Circle the number with a two in the ones place.

(Have children turn to the next page.)

9. Miko has nine balloons for a birthday party. She gives away two of the balloons. How many balloons does she have left? Write the number on the line.

10. Look at the shapes. Which is a square? Color in the square.

11. Look at the shapes. Which one is a cylinder? Draw a circle around the cylinder.

12. Look at the clock. The minute hand shows how many minutes past the hour? Circle the number of minutes.

13. Look at the row of clocks. Which clock shows 9:30? Circle the clock that shows 9:30.

(Have children turn to the next page.)

14. Look at the pencil. The bar under the pencil shows one inch. About how many inches long is the pencil? Circle the number.

15–16. Find the answer to each problem. Write your answers.

17. Look at the pictures. If you weigh a pair of scissors, a brick, a crayon, and an apple, which thing will weigh most? Circle the picture of the thing that weighs most.

18. Look at the coins. What is the value of the coins? Write the amount on the line.

19. Ricardo has 25 cents. He spends 20 cents to buy a yo-yo. Which coin shows how much money Ricardo has left? Draw a circle around the coin.

20. Four friends go frog hunting. They keep a record of how many frogs are found by Jess, Cam, Ira, and Ali. Look at the tally marks for each friend. Circle the name of the person who found the most frogs.

1.  ___ ___

2.

| 18 | 19 | 20 | |

3.

2, 4, 6, 8, 10, _____, _____

4.    5   6   7   8

5. 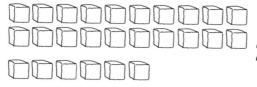   21   30   16   26

6.

Sunday   Tuesday   Wednesday   Saturday

7.

January   March   October   December

8.

23   30   42   20

9.

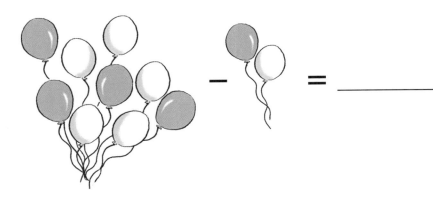 = _____

10.

11.

12.

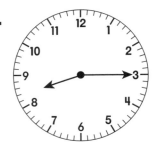   10   15   20   25

13.

NAME_____

14.

├─────┤ .
  1 inch

| 1 | 2 | 3 | 4 |

15.   7
        +4

16.   15
         −8

17.

18.

_____

19.

20.

Jess	Cam	Ira	Ali
////	//// /	////	//// ///

1. △ ▧

2. 21

3. 12, 14

4. 7

5. 26

6. Sunday

7. December

8. 42

9. 7

10. 1st picture (square)

11. 3rd picture (can)

12. 15

13. 4th picture (9:30)

14. 3

15. 11

16. 7

17. 2nd picture (brick)

18. 23¢ or $0.23

19. 2nd picture (nickel)

20. Ali

Tested Skills	Item Numbers	Every Day Counts Element(s)
Grouping and counting	2, 3	Calendar, Clock, Counting Tape and Ten Grids, Daily Depositor
Quantities, numerals, and place value	4, 5, 8	Counting Tape and Ten Grids, Daily Depositor, Number Builder
Days and months	6, 7	Calendar
Patterns	1	Calendar
Geometric shapes	10, 11	Calendar
Money and time	12, 13, 18, 19	Clock, Coin Counter
Measuring and comparing	14, 17	Measurement
Solving problems	9, 15, 16	Number Builder
Interpreting data	20	Graph

Read each item aloud. (Have children look at the first page.)

1. Look at the stars in the box. How many stars are in the box? Draw a circle around the number that tells how many stars.

2. Look at the numbers in the boxes. What number comes next? Write the number in the box.

3. Look at the numbers: five, ten, fifteen, twenty . . . . What number comes next? Write the number on the line.

4. Look at the salt shakers. Each one needs a pepper shaker to go with it. Which group has exactly one pepper shaker for each salt shaker? Circle the group that has one pepper shaker for each salt shaker.

5. Look at the names of the days: Tuesday, Wednesday, Thursday, Friday. Which day comes next after Monday? Circle the name of the day that comes next after Monday.

6. Look at the names of the months: May, July, September, October. Which month comes next after August? Circle the name of the month that comes next after August.

7. Look at the shapes. Which shape is a triangle? Color in the triangle.

(Have children turn to the next page.)

8. Look at the numbers. Which number is greater than 19? Circle the number greater than 19.

9. Look at the numbers. Which number has a three in the ones place? Circle the number that has a three in the ones place.

10. Look at the numbers. Which number is ten more than seven? Circle the number that is ten more than seven.

11. Look at the shapes. They make a pattern. What shape comes next? Draw the shape that comes next.

12. Look at the sets of hearts. Which set has one less than nine? Circle the set of hearts with one less than nine.

13. Look at the groups of kittens. Three kittens were looking out the window. Five more kittens came to sit with them. How many kittens are there altogether? Write your answer.

14–15. Find the answer to each problem. Write your answers.

(Have children turn to the next page.)

16. Look at the coins. What is the value of the coins? Write the amount on the line.

17. Look at the square clock (on the left). The hour hand points to what number? Write the number on the line.

18. Look at the round clock (on the right). The minute hand shows how many minutes past the hour? Write the number of minutes on the line.

19. Look at the package of candy. There is one candy above the package. About how many of these candies are lined up in the package? Circle the number.

20. Look at the graph of favorite fruits. It shows how many children picked each fruit. Which fruit was picked by the most children? Circle the fruit that was picked most.

NAME _____

1. 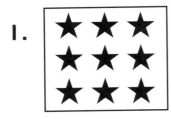   7   8   9   10

2.

| 15 | 16 | 17 | |

3.

5, 10, 15, 20, _____

4.

5.

Tuesday   Wednesday   Thursday   Friday

6.

May   July   September   October

7.

8.

| 10 | 12 | 15 | 20 |

9.

| 23 | 24 | 27 | 30 |

10.

| 16 | 17 | 19 | 27 |

11.

 _____

12.

13.

  _____

14.
$$\begin{array}{r} 6 \\ +\ 4 \\ \hline \end{array}$$

15.
$$\begin{array}{r} 12 \\ -\ 9 \\ \hline \end{array}$$

16.   _____

17. 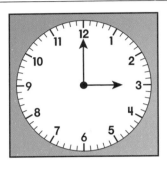 _____

18. 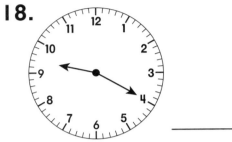 _____

19.    1   2   4   6

20.

Favorite Fruits

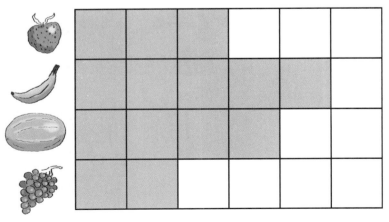

Number of Children

1. 9
2. 18
3. 25
4. 3rd picture (7 shakers)
5. Tuesday
6. September
7. 2nd picture (triangle)

8. 20
9. 23
10. 17
11.
12. 3rd picture (8 hearts)
13. 8

14. 10
15. 3
16. 12¢ or $0.12
17. 3
18. 20
19. 4
20. banana

Tested Skills	Item Numbers	Every Day Counts Element(s)
Grouping and counting	2, 3	Calendar, Clock, Counting Tape and Ten Grids, Daily Depositor
Quantities and numerals	1, 8, 12	Counting Tape and Ten Grids, Daily Depositor, Number Builder
Days and months	5, 6	Calendar
Patterns	11	Calendar
Geometric shapes	7	Calendar
One-to-one correspondence	4	Counting Tape and Ten Grids, Number Builder
Place value	9, 10	Counting Tape and Ten Grids, Daily Depositor
Money and time	16, 17, 18	Clock, Coin Counter
Measuring and comparing length	19	Measurement
Solving problems	13, 14, 15	Number Builder
Interpreting graphs	20	Graph

Read each item aloud. (Have children look at the first page.)

1. Look at the pattern of shapes. What shape comes next? Draw the shape that comes next.

2. Look at the numbers: one, three, five, seven . . . . What should the next three numbers be? Write the next three numbers on the lines.

3. Look at the numbers: ten, twenty, thirty . . . . What two numbers come next? Write the next two numbers on the lines.

4. Look at the puppies. Each one needs a bone. Which group has exactly one bone for each puppy? Circle the group that has exactly one bone for each puppy.

5. Look at the names of the days: Sunday, Monday, Friday, Saturday. Which day comes next after Thursday? Circle the name of the day that comes next after Thursday.

6. Look at the names of the months: January, April, June, November. Which month comes next after March? Circle the name of the month that comes after March.

7. Look at the flowers. Each flower has petals. How many petals are there in all? Circle the number that tells how many petals.

(Have children turn to the next page.)

8. Look at the shapes. Which shape has a circle at both ends? Circle the shape that has a circle at both ends.

9. Look at the numbers. Which number is greater than 27? Circle the number that is greater than 27.

10. Look at the numbers. Which number is ten less than 25? Circle the number that is less than 25.

11. Look at the numbers. Which number has a one in the tens place? Circle the number that has a one in the tens place.

12. Look at the coins. What is the value of the coins? Write the amount on the line.

13. Look at the picture of the toy horse. Benjy wants to buy this toy horse. It costs ten cents. He pays for the toy horse with a quarter. How much money should he get back? Write the amount on the line.

14–15. Find the answer to each problem. Write your answers.

(Have children turn to the next page.)

16. Look at the socks. If you put all the socks together in pairs, how many pairs of socks will there be? Write the number of pairs.

17. Look at the time shown on the round clock. Which digital clock shows the same time? Circle the digital clock that shows the same time.

18. Look at the number expressions. Which is the same as nine? Circle the expression for nine.

19. Look at the fish. Eleven fish are playing together. Then three of the fish swim away. How many fish are left? Write your answer on the line.

20. Look at the graph. It shows the number of books read by Kim, Deb, Ron, and Max. Who read the most books? Circle the name of the child who read the most books.

1.   _____

2. 1, 3, 5, 7, _____, _____, _____

3. 10, 20, 30, _____, _____

4.

5.

Sunday   Monday   Friday   Saturday

6.

January   April   June   November

7. 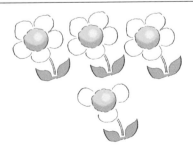   4   15   18   20

8.

9. 30   18   9   26

10. 10   24   15   20

11. 21   12   1   31

12.   _____

13.   _____

14.   8
   +9
  _____

15.   15
   −4
  _____

16.

17.

18.

$$3 + 5 \qquad 7 + 1 \qquad 5 + 4 \qquad 2 + 6$$

19.  _____

20.

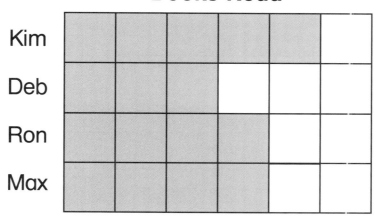

Books Read

	Number of Books					
Kim						
Deb						
Ron						
Max						

Number of Books

SPRING TEST ANSWER KEY

1.

2. 9, 11, 13

3. 40, 50

4. 2nd picture (6 bones)

5. Friday

6. April

7. 18

8. 4th picture (cylinder)

9. 30

10. 15

11. 12

12. 18¢ or $0.18

13. 15¢

14. 17

15. 11

16. 5

17. 5:00

18. 5 + 4

19. 8

20. Kim

Tested Skills	Item Numbers	Every Day Counts Element(s)
Grouping and counting	2, 3, 16	Calendar, Clock, Counting Tape and Ten Grids, Daily Depositor
Quantities and numerals	7, 9, 18	Counting Tape and Ten Grids, Daily Depositor, Number Builder
Days and months	5, 6	Calendar
Patterns	1	Calendar
One-to-one correspondence	4	Counting Tape and Ten Grids, Number Builder
Geometric shapes	8	Calendar
Place value	10, 11	Counting Tape and Ten Grids, Daily Depositor,
Money and time	12, 13, 17	Clock, Coin Counter
Solving problems	14, 15, 19	Number Builder
Interpreting graphs	20	Graph

Read each item aloud. (Have children look at the first page.)

1. Look at the pattern of shapes. What should the next two shapes be? Draw the two shapes that come next.

2. Look at the numbers in the boxes. What number comes next? Write the number in the box.

3. Look at the numbers: ten, twelve, fourteen, sixteen . . . . What numbers come next? Write the next two numbers on the lines.

4. Look at the ladybugs. How many ladybugs are there? Draw a circle around the number that tells how many ladybugs.

5. Look at the boxes. How many boxes are there? Draw a circle around the number that tells how many boxes.

6. Look at the names of the days: Sunday, Monday, Thursday, Friday. Which day comes just before Saturday? Circle the name of the day that comes just before Saturday.

7. Look at the names of the months: February, March, May, June. Which month comes next after April? Circle the name of the month that comes next after April.

(Have children turn to the next page.)

8. Look at the numbers. Which number has a three in the ones place? Circle the number with a three in the ones place.

9. Jenna has twelve packs of gum. She gives away four of the packs of gum. How many packs of gum does she have left? Write the number on the line.

10. Look at the pictures. Which is a triangle? Draw an X on the triangle.

11. Look at the shapes. Which one is a cone? Draw a circle around the cone.

12. Look at the clock. The minute hand shows how many minutes past the hour? Circle the number of minutes.

13. Look at the row of clocks. Which clock shows 10:25? Circle the clock that shows 10:25.

(Have children turn to the next page.)

14. Look at the bead necklace. The bar under the necklace shows one inch. About how many inches long is the necklace? Circle the number.

15–16. Find the answer to each problem. Write your answers.

17. Look at the pictures. If you weigh a pack of crayons, an apple, a sandwich, and a pitcher of lemonade, which thing will weigh most? Circle the picture of the thing that weighs most.

18. Look at the coins. What is the value of the coins? Write the amount on the line.

19. Danny has 25 cents. He spends 15 cents to buy some gum. Which coin shows how much money Danny has left? Draw a circle around the coin.

20. Four friends go to the Games Fair at school. They keep a record of how many games are won by Bim, Kat, Tina, and Ray. Look at the tally marks for each friend. Circle the name of the person who won the most games.

NAME_____

1.

 ___ ___

2.

| 27 | 28 | 29 | |

3.

10, 12, 14, 16, _____, _____

4.

   6   7   8   9

5.

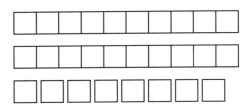   18   28   20   30

6.

Sunday   Monday   Thursday   Friday

7.

February   March   May   June

NAME_____

8.

43   30   24   34

9.   –  = _____

10.

11.

12.    10   15   20   25

13.

14.

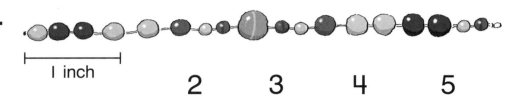

| inch

2   3   4   5

15.

6
+5

16.

14
−9

17.

18.

        _____

19.

20.

Bim	Kat	Tina	Ray
卌I	卌II	IIII	卌

1.

2. 30

3. 18, 20

4. 9

5. 28

6. Friday

7. May

8. 43

9. 8

10. 3rd picture (pennant)

11. 1st picture (cone)

12. 25

13. 2nd picture (10:25)

14. 5

15. 11

16. 5

17. 4th picture
(pitcher of lemonade)

18. 27¢ or $0.27

19. 3rd picture (dime)

20. 2nd picture (Kat)

Tested Skills	Item Numbers	Every Day Counts Element(s)
Grouping and counting	2, 3	Calendar, Clock, Counting Tape and Ten Grids, Daily Depositor
Quantities, numerals, and place value	4, 5, 8	Counting Tape and Ten Grids, Daily Depositor, Number Builder
Days and months	6, 7	Calendar
Patterns	1	Calendar
Geometric shapes	10, 11	Calendar
Money and time	12, 13, 18, 19	Clock, Coin Counter
Measuring and comparing	14, 17	Measurement
Solving problems	9, 15, 16	Number Builder
Interpreting data	20	Graph

TEACHING RESOURCES

TR1 Calendar Record

TR2 Date Cards

TR3 Calendar Cutouts A

TR4 Calendar Cutouts B

TR5 0–9 Domino Halves

TR6 Double Domino Blanks

TR7 Dotted Domino Halves

TR8 Ten Grid Number Cards

TR9 Ten Grids

TR10 0–9 Digit Cards

TR11 0–9 Numeral Dot Cards

TR12 Clock

TR13 A.M./P.M. Chart

TR14 Birthday Package and Gift Tags

TR15 Graph

TR16 Weather/Shoe Markers

TR17 Inch Squared Paper

TR18 Centimeter Squared Paper

TR19 Circle Array

TR20 Hundred Chart

TR21 Blank Hundred Chart

TR22 Play Money—Coin Cards

TR23 Coin Counter Record

TR24 Coin Comparing Cards

TR25 Piggy Bank/Purse backgrounds

TR26 Cookie Jar/Box Backgrounds

TR27 Sample Vocabulary A

TR28 Sample Vocabulary B

DAYS OF THE WEEK IN SPANISH

Sunday	domingo
Monday	lunes
Tuesday	martes
Wednesday	miércoles
Thursday	jueves
Friday	viernes
Saturday	sábado

NUMBERS THROUGH 31 IN SPANISH

one	uno
two	dos
three	tres
four	cuatro
five	cinco
six	seis
seven	siete
eight	ocho
nine	nueve
ten	diez
eleven	once
twelve	doce
thirteen	trece
fourteen	catorce
fifteen	quince
sixteen	diez y seis
seventeen	diez y siete
eighteen	diez y ocho
nineteen	diez y nueve
twenty	viente
twenty-one	viente y uno
twenty-two	viente y dos
twenty-three	viente y tres
twenty-four	viente y cuatro
twenty-five	viente y cinco
twenty-six	viente y seis
twenty-seven	viente y siete
twenty-eight	viente y ocho
twenty-nine	viente y nueve
thirty	treinta
thirty-one	treinta y uno

month _____

Sunday	Monday	Tuesday	Wednesday	Thursday	Friday	Saturday

1	2	3	4	5
6	7	8	9	10
11	12	13	14	15
16	17	18	19	20
21	22	23	24	25
26	27	28	29	30
	31			

TR3 Calendar Cutouts A

TR4   Calendar Cutouts B

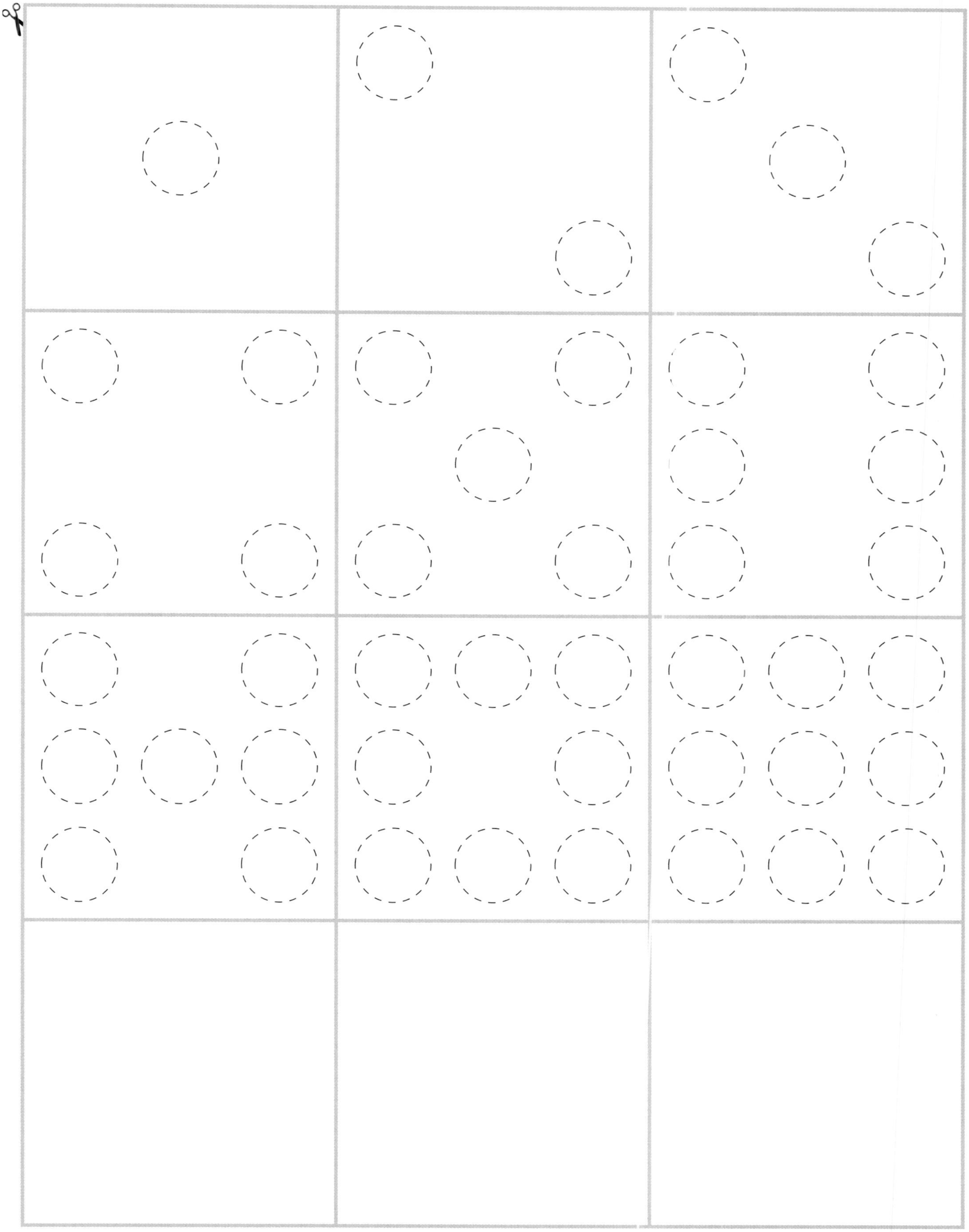

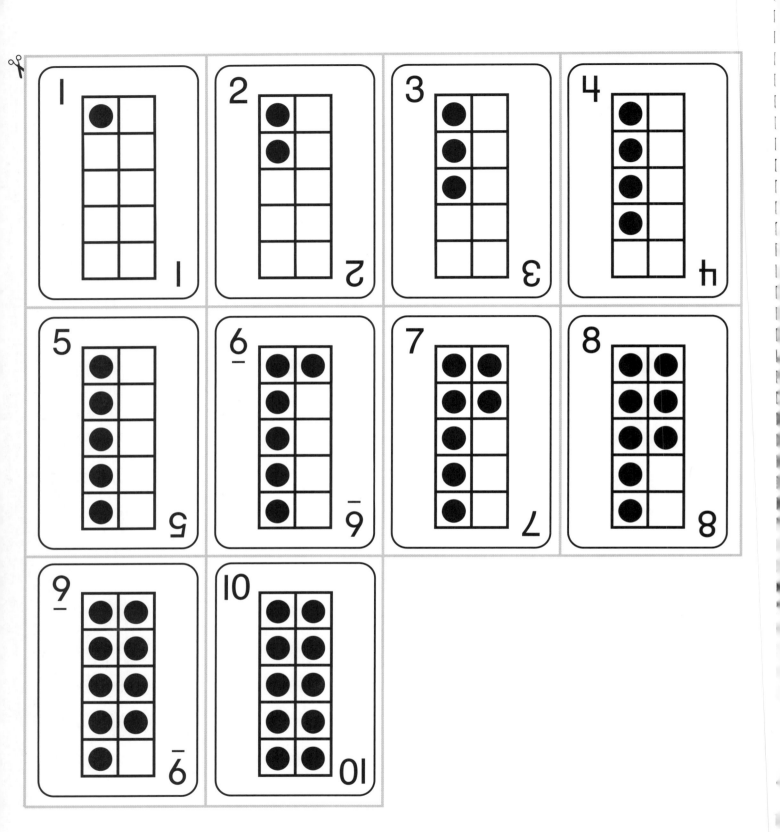

0 1 2 3 4

5 6 7 8 9

0 1 2 3 4

5 6 7 8 9

0

1
•

2
• •

3
• • •

4
• • • •

5
• • • • •

6
• • • •
• •

7
• • • •
• • •

8
• • • •
• • • •

9
• • • • •
• • • •

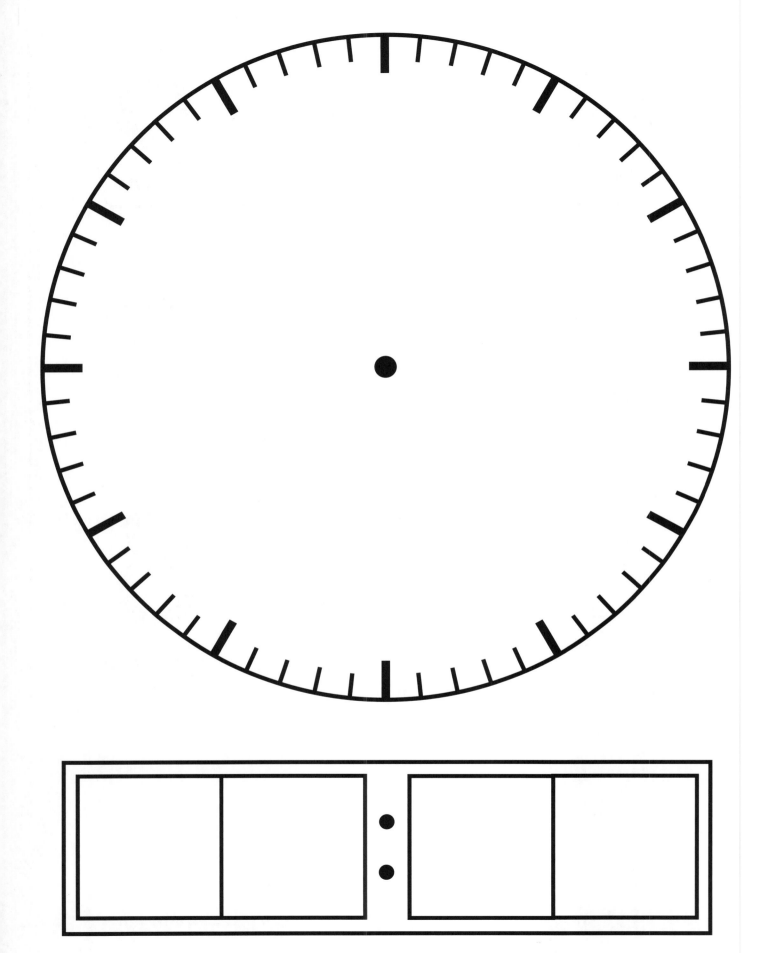

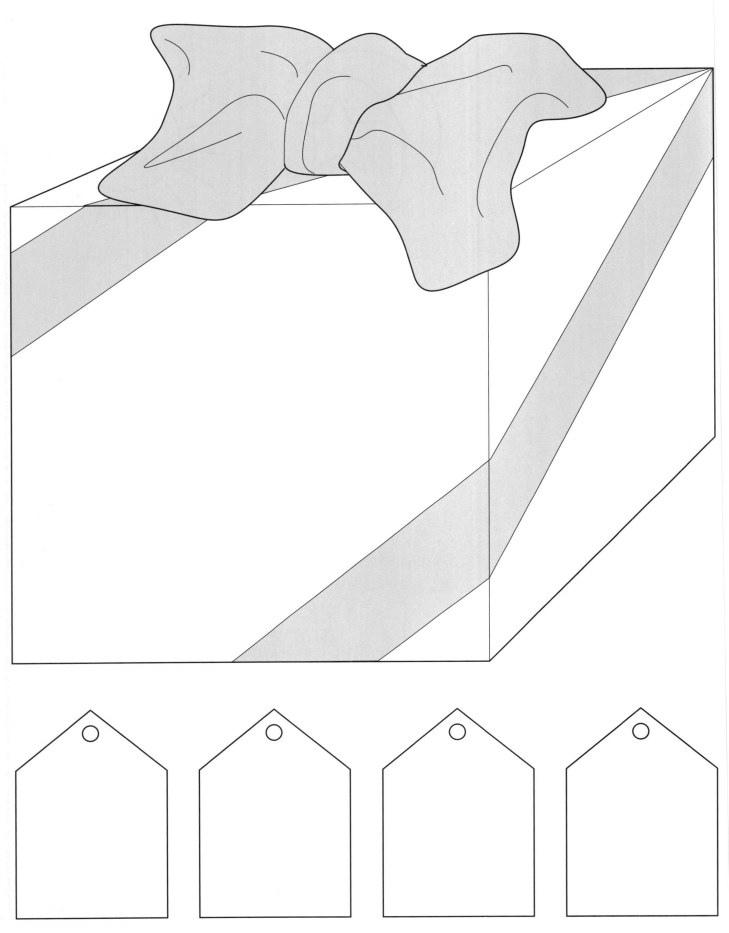

TR17 Inch Squared Paper

TR19 Circle Array

1	2	3	4	5	6	7	8	9	10
11	12	13	14	15	16	17	18	19	20
21	22	23	24	25	26	27	28	29	30
31	32	33	34	35	36	37	38	39	40
41	42	43	44	45	46	47	48	49	50
51	52	53	54	55	56	57	58	59	60
61	62	63	64	65	66	67	68	69	70
71	72	73	74	75	76	77	78	79	80
81	82	83	84	85	86	87	88	89	90
91	92	93	94	95	96	97	98	99	100

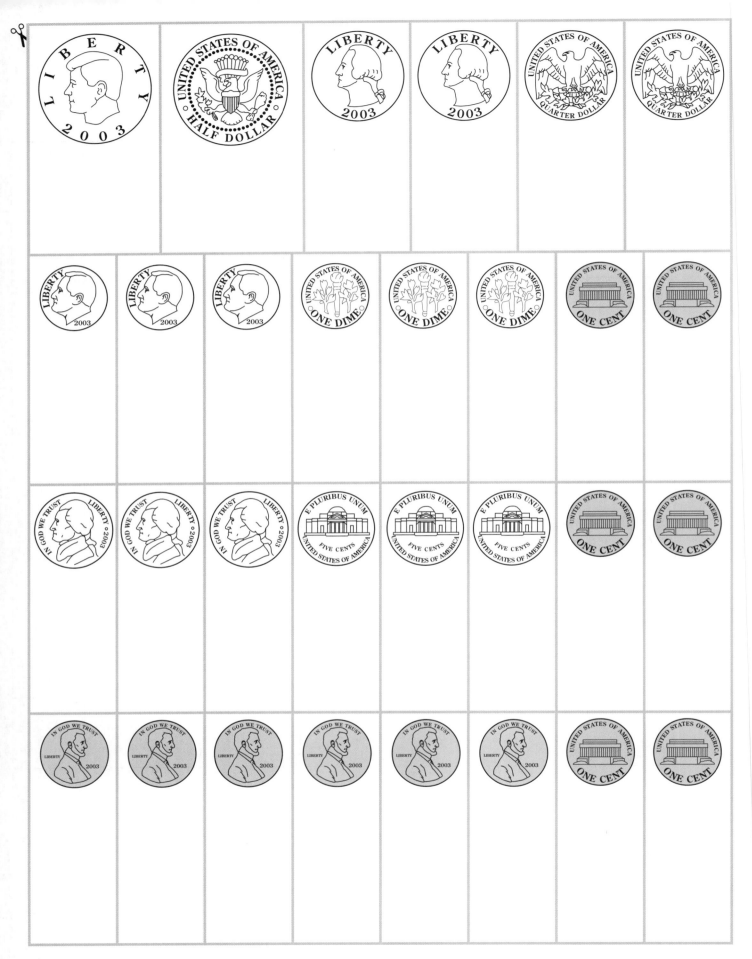

Today we have

$ _____ or _____ ¢

TR25 Piggy Bank/Purse Backgrounds

triangle
A shape with 3 straight sides.

cylinder
A can shape.

rectangle
A shape with 4 straight sides and 4 square corners.

sphere
A ball shape.

square
A shape with 4 straight sides all the same length and 4 square corners.

face
A flat side of a 3-D shape.

face

circle
A perfectly round shape.

symmetry
A shape that can be folded so the two halves match exactly has symmetry.

line of symmetry

rectangular solid
A box shape with 6 faces that are rectangles.

pattern
Something that changes in the same way over and over.

cube
A box shape with 6 faces that are squares.

A.M.
Morning times before noon.

cone
A 3-D shape with a point at one end and a circle on the other end.

P.M.
Afternoon and evening times before midnight.

These might be used to accompany discussions, to build individual student word banks, or to enlarge for a Word Wall.

TR27   Sample Vocabulary A

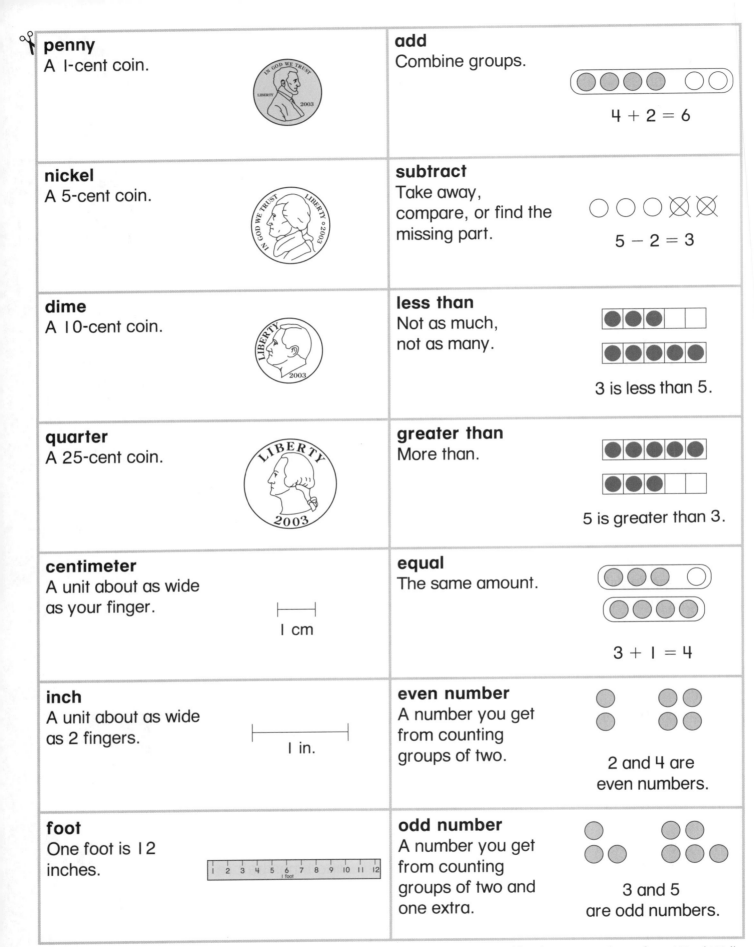

penny
A 1-cent coin.

add
Combine groups.

$4 + 2 = 6$

nickel
A 5-cent coin.

subtract
Take away, compare, or find the missing part.

$5 - 2 = 3$

dime
A 10-cent coin.

less than
Not as much, not as many.

3 is less than 5.

quarter
A 25-cent coin.

greater than
More than.

5 is greater than 3.

centimeter
A unit about as wide as your finger.

1 cm

equal
The same amount.

$3 + 1 = 4$

inch
A unit about as wide as 2 fingers.

1 in.

even number
A number you get from counting groups of two.

2 and 4 are even numbers.

foot
One foot is 12 inches.

1 2 3 4 5 6 7 8 9 10 11 12
1 foot

odd number
A number you get from counting groups of two and one extra.

3 and 5 are odd numbers.

These might be used to accompany discussions, to build individual student word banks, or to enlarge for a Word Wall.

TR28 Sample Vocabulary B

INDEX

A

Addition

basic facts, 21–23, 24–27, 36–38, 40–42, 50–51, 64–65, 66–67, 75–77, 89–90, 104–105, 107–108, 117–118, 130–131

concepts, 21–23, 24–27, 36–38, 40–42, 50–51, 55–57, 64–65, 75–77, 89–90, 104–105, 107–108, 117–118, 130–131

models, 21–23, 24–27, 36–38, 40–42, 50–51, 55–57, 64–65, 66–67, 75–77, 89–90, 104–105, 107–108, 117–118, 130–131

number combinations, 21–23, 24–27, 34–35, 36–38, 40–42, 50–51, 55–57, 64–65, 68–69, 75–77, 89–90, 92–93, 104–105, 107–109, 117–118, 121–122, 130–131

repeated, 88

Algebra

algebraic thinking, 18–20, 26–27, 34–36, 48–49, 62–64, 87–90, 102–103, 116–117, 128–129

equations, 21–23, 36–38, 50–51, 64–65, 75–76, 89–90, 104–105, 117–118, 130–131

expressions, 21–23, 36–38, 68–69, 89–90, 104–105

functions, 87–88, 102–103

patterns. *See* Number patterns.

Assessment

assessment materials, 137–157

ongoing assessment questions, 18, 21, 24, 28, 30, 34, 36, 38, 40, 43, 44, 48, 50, 52, 54, 55, 57, 59, 62, 64, 66, 68, 69, 70, 74, 75, 77, 79, 80, 81, 83, 87, 89, 91, 92, 95, 97, 98, 102, 104, 105, 107, 108, 110, 111, 116, 117, 119, 121, 122, 123, 128, 130, 131, 133, 134

B

Basic facts, 21–23, 24–27, 36–38, 40–42, 50–51, 64–65, 66–67, 75–77, 89–90, 104–105, 107–108, 117–118, 130–131

Benchmarks. *See* Counting.

C

Calculator, 57, 80, 98–99, 110, 123, 133

Calendar, 18–20, 34–35, 48–49, 62–63, 74–75, 87–88, 102–103, 116–117, 128–129

Capacity, 105–106

Circle. *See* Two-dimensional shapes.

Classifying

objects by attribute, 51

triangles, 48–49

two-dimensional shapes, 34–35, 48–49, 87–88, 116–117

three-dimensional shapes, 62–64, 128–130, 134–135

Clock, 28–29, 43, 57–59, 70–71, 81–82, 97–98, 110–111

Coin. *See* Money.

Communication

discussion questions, 19–20, 26–27, 31, 34–35, 37, 39, 41–42, 44–45, 49, 55, 56, 58, 63, 65, 67, 68, 69, 71, 76–77, 79, 81, 82, 83, 87–88, 90, 91, 96, 97, 98, 99, 102–103, 104–105, 106, 109, 110, 112, 116, 120, 123, 124–125, 128–129, 131, 135

sample dialogues, 19, 22–23, 29, 37–38, 40, 51, 53, 58, 63, 66–67, 76, 78, 92, 93–94, 107–108, 118–119, 120

Comparison

alike/different, 18–20, 34–36, 49, 62–64, 123–125

compare measurements. *See* Capacity, Length, and Weight.

greater than/less than/equal to, 54–55

more/fewer/same, 38–40, 54–55, 105–106, 123–125

Cone. *See* Three-dimensional shapes.

Counting

by fives, 24–27, 28–30, 40–42, 43, 55–56, 57–58, 59, 68, 69, 70–71, 79, 80. 1–82, 92–94, 96, 97–98, 107, 108–109, 110, 121,122, 131–132, 133

by ones, 24–27, 28–30, 34–35, 40–42, 43, 48–49, 54, 55–56, 59, 66–67, 68, 77–78, 79, 91, 92, 107, 121–122, 133

by tens, 24–27, 40–42, 52–53, 55–57, 66–67, 68,79, 91, 92, 107, 121, 131–132

Home involvement, 135

Hundredth Day, 86, 92–94

Inch, 54–55

Isosceles triangle, 48–49

Length
customary units, 54–55
height (taller/shorter), 105–106
length (shorter/longer), 38–40, 54–55, 86

Literature
bibliography, 136

Logical reasoning, 18–20, 34–35, 48–49, 62–63, 74–75, 87–88, 102–103, 116–117, 128–129

Manipulatives
classroom objects, 38–40, 116–117
real-world objects, 38–40, 52–53

Measurement
customary, 54–55
estimating, 38–40, 54–55, 86, 105–106, 119–121
length. *See* Length.
measurement comparisons
    heavy/heavier/heaviest, 119–121
    large/larger, 119–121
    long/longer/longest, 38–40, 54–55, 86, 123–125
    right/left, 74–75
    short/shorter/shortest, 38–40, 123–125
nonstandard units, 38–40, 52–53, 86, 105–106, 119–121

pan balance, 119–121
temperature. *See* Temperature.
time. *See* Time.
weight. *See* Weight.

Mental math, 24–27, 30–31, 40–42, 48–49, 57–59, 62–64, 68–70, 87–90, 95–96, 102–105, 108–109, 116–119, 128–130, 133

Models. *See* Manipulatives.

Money
dime, 80–81, 95–96, 102–103, 108–109, 133
nickel, 55–59, 69–70, 80–81, 95–96, 102–103, 108–109, 133
penny, 55–59, 69–70, 80–81, 95–96, 102–103, 108–109, 133
quarter, 80–81, 95–96, 108–109, 133

Multiplication
multiples, 87–88

Number line, 24–27, 40–42, 55–57, 68–69, 79, 92–94, 107–108, 121–122, 131–132

Number
combinations, 21–27, 34–36, 55–57, 68–69, 80–81, 92–94, 107–108, 121–122
comparing and ordering, 18–20, 30–31, 34–36, 40–42, 48–49, 55–57, 62–64, 68–69, 74–75, 87–88, 91–92, 102–103, 105–106, 116–117, 123–125, 128–132
even, 87–88, 98–99
matching a numeral to a quantity, 18–20, 21–27, 34–38, 48–49, 52–53, 62–64, 66–67, 77–78, 86–88, 91–92, 98–99, 102–103, 116–117, 128–131
odd, 55–57, 87–88, 98–99
patterns, 18–20, 24–27, 34–35, 40–42, 48–49, 62–63, 74–75, 79, 87–88, 98–99, 102–103, 116–117, 128–129, 128–130
reading/writing, 30–31, 48–49, 62–64, 66–67, 74–75, 77–78, 87–88, 91–92, 102–103, 116–117, 128–130

Number sense, 18–20, 24–27, 40–42, 79, 92–94, 107–108, 121–122, 131–132

Operations. *See* Addition, Subtraction, *or* Multiplication.

Ordering. *See* Number.

Pattern
identifying, 18–20, 24–27, 34–35, 40–42, 48–49, 55–57, 62–63, 74–75, 79, 87–88, 102–103, 116–117, 128–129

predicting, 18–20, 24–27, 34–35, 40–42, 48–49 55–57, 62–63, 74–75, 79, 87–88, 102–103, 116–117, 128–129

Place value
decimal, 57–59, 69–70, 80–81, 95–96, 108–109

models, 24–27, 36–38, 40–42, 52–53, 66–67, 80–81, 86, 91–96, 107–109, 121–122, 131–132

through hundreds, 24–27, 36–38, 40–42, 52–53, 55–57, 66–67, 86, 91–94, 107–108, 121–122, 131–132

through thousands, 86

Plane shapes. *See* Two-dimensional shapes.

Polygon. *See* Two-dimensional shapes.

Probability
event, 34–36, 66–67, 87–88

likelihood of an event, 34–36, 55–57, 66–67, 70, 87–88

organizing experiment outcomes, 55–57, 66–67, 70, 87–88

performing simple experiments, 34–36, 55–57, 66–67, 70, 87–88

prediction and, 34–36, 87–88

Problem solving
act it out, 21–30, 34–36, 57–59, 62–64, 66–67, 79, 80–81, 86–88, 95–96, 108–109, 133

compare strategies, 24–27, 34–36, 40–42, 48–49, 62–64, 66–67, 95–96, 133

find a pattern, 24–27, 48–49, 68–69, 74–75, 121–122

guess and check, 21–23, 36–38, 80–81, 119–121, 133

logical reasoning, 30–31, 34–36, 80–81, 95–96, 133

make a list, 80–81, 89–90, 133

number stories, 21–23, 36–38, 48–51, 64–65, 68–69, 80–81, 89–90, 95–96, 104–105, 117–118, 130–131

Quadrilateral
rectangle, 18–20, 34–36, 48–49

rhombus, 116–117

square, 18–20, 34–36, 48–49, 134–135

Quantity
add and subtract, 21–27, 36–38, 40–42, 50–51, 55–59, 64–67, 75–79, 89–90, 91–92, 104–105, 108–109, 117–118, 130–131

compare and order, 24–27, 34–36, 40–42, 44–45, 55–57, 62–64, 66–67, 77–79, 83, 87–90, 91–92, 107–109, 116–117, 119–121

match with numeral, 18–27, 34–38, 40–42, 48–49, 50–53, 64–67, 77–79, 86, 89–90, 91–92, 98–99, 104–105, 117–118, 130–131

part-whole relationships, 21–23, 24–27, 34–36, 36–38, 40–42, 50–51, 55–56, 64–65, 68, 75–76, 79, 89–90, 92–94, 104, 107, 117–118, 121, 130, 131

Reasoning. *See* Logical reasoning.

Rectangle. *See* Two-dimensional shapes.

Rectangular prism. *See* Three-dimensional shapes.

Referents
time, 43, 70

length, 54–55, 70–71

Right angle. *See* Square corner.

Rotation (turn), 116–117